AF405358

KAMENKO KESAR

My Wife is Always Right

PART ONE

Man and Woman

All Men are Phenomenal Lovers

It is a truth universally acknowledged that all men are good in bed. That is, of course, until we have sex for the first time. Therein lies the rub. Well, it's not our fault. Women, almost certainly inadvertently, crush our fragile egos. And we men drag that pain, like a ball and chain, from relationship to relationship in an endless tangle of utter disaster.

Take me, for example. I was born a phenomenal lover. But then I met a girl who wore a lovely perfume to which I proved allergic. Each time I lay down next to her and pressed myself to her lips, I sneezed into her neck instead of kissing her. She didn't notice, of course, because I withheld this projectile sneeze and shifted its momentum inwards, nearly blowing my ears off. The only sound I permitted to ooze forth was the expulsion of air between my front teeth that produced a sound not unlike the voice of a villainous mouse. Ussssssssh.

I once excavated one of her erogenous zones by accident while using this technique. Excited, I rushed at her but, en route, I still sneezed into her neck. I calculated that it would be wiser to retreat from her body and perfume, so I pushed my body up, high above her, far enough away. But when I found myself about to sneeze again, I no longer had a neck against which to cushion the nasal explosion. I was too far from her skin, the blanket was on the floor, and I couldn't put my hand in front of my mouth and nose, because if I raised my hands, I would fall on top of her.

Time slows down in case of emergencies, and the situation, running in slow motion before me, appeared hopeless.

Luckily, the babe closed her eyes for a moment. The Fates had spoken. I relaxed and surrendered to destiny. My pupils rolled up into my head. At the last moment, I buried my face between her beautiful boobs. I sneezed through my closed mouth and released the already familiar "ussssssssh."

The girl opened her eyes, smiled up at me, and looked down at her breasts. She stared at them for a while. Then she looked up at me and said, in surprise, "I've never met anyone with green goodge before."

I Have Limited Multitasking

We men are multi-taskers. That is indisputable, proven and provable at all times.

We can meander in our BMW between slow cars while, at the same time, chewing out the car on the left who is not keeping adequate track of what's happening on the road. We can unscrew a water pipe and, at the same time, explain to our son the importance of manual dexterity. Let it be said that I can place my dish in the dishwasher and, at the very same moment, berate my beloved wife with the observation that three plates cannot go into the same slot in said dishwasher. Well, comes the retort, they do all fit because she crammed them in there successfully, but my point is that they shouldn't.

That's not all. Men can even erotically engage with their lover's breasts while thinking about that email we should really have replied to that lurks in our inbox. Well, not me. A colleague. We can pee in the snow and demonstrate our manual dexterity by writing our name with it. Well, not me. My bladder is too small to write out "Kamenko Kesar."

Yes, we are great multi-taskers. Invincible. Entirely self-sufficient (almost). Unfortunately, this multitasking has one rather awkward limitation. It works only if one of our activities is physical and the other is mental. Changing/explaining. Cleaning/berating. Peeing/writing. Caressing/replying by email. Additional corporeal actions lead to trouble. For example, it's tricky to drive a car and crack walnuts at the same time. Or caress our beloved with both hands. This doesn't work for men. Well, aside from me. When I had one hand on her breast and the other against her cheek, I could caress her in two locations simultaneously. She would be likely, in such an instance, to inquire as to what the fuck I was trying to achieve by making circular motions with my fingers against her left cheek, but that was my secret. What does she care?

In short, two physical actions do not go together. Nature has made men focused when it comes to actions. So it was in the olden days. We ran in front of a lion and at the same time wondered "Why me?" Or, in our youth, we would dance with a girl while praying fiercely that she would touch our wang. Well, not me. A colleague.

Nature knows what She's doing. She has made certain that, in certain exceptional cases, it is possible to physically multi-task. We can, thank goodness, weave around traffic on a busy road while excavating our left nostril for veins of gold while shouting "Die, motherfucker!" to the asshole who's driving 60 in the passing lane. Nature, in her infinite wisdom, has bequeathed unto us the ability to fix plumbing under the sink while simultaneously scratching our balls and...and...explaining the ways of the world to our son. We can, if the wind shifts in the right direction, caress our beloved wife on both breasts. At the same time. Provided that we're caressing in the same direction and at the same rhythm, of course. Heck, when I was younger I was even able to dance with her and hold onto her ass at the same time.

Being the Perfect Man is a Cornucopia of Suffering

It was shortly before lunch and getting uncomfortably hot outside. I was sitting in the shade of the balcony of a pleasant hotel in the middle of Opatija, on the northern Croatian coast. Below me, a large terrace was dotted with round tables. A hedge ran behind the terrace. There were also stairs to the promenade and, behind them, a path to the beach and the majestic sea stretching into the horizon. This was what I needed and also what I expected. I wanted to close my eyes and clear out the broom cupboard of my thoughts, to quench the excitement of the hectic work days behind me, to focus on myself and to find peace. I would forget about the people around me, their activities, their frustrations. I leaned back and placed my hands luxuriantly behind my neck, took a deep breath and tried to gather in this moment of infinity, peace and benevolent coexistence.

And then they appeared on the stairs.

The hotel terrace fell silent as they arrived. Both were around thirty, she was in the shortest and tightest white skirt in creation, a bright blouse, a white jacket and the longest whitest boots I've ever seen, nearly scraped by her long, so very long, straight brown hair. She wore oversized sunglasses and a matching set of oversized boobies. He had stepped out of a catalogue: short hair, broad shoulders, a face chiseled from Carrera marble, wearing sunglasses, a designer t-shirt, sweater, jacket, a scarf dashingly draped around his neck, striped trousers and brown leather shoes, all offset by an oversized silver watch.

They sat at a table I could see from my balcony without having to move. She turned her back to me, and he looked up at me for a moment. I know this type of man, I thought. Well enough that, I immediately realized, my quest for a moment of infinity and coexistence had just fallen into the water.

There they were, both beautiful and starry, on the terrace of this luxury hotel. My guess was that they'd driven down from the cloudy capitol in a white Audi. That they'd just thrown on their most beautiful matching clothes that morning before stepping out from their fully-purchased, mortgage-free home and presenting themselves unto the common people.

The sun strengthened and the beautiful couple sat, motionless it seemed from my vantage, at the table. Well, almost motionless. The man toyed with his sunglasses and secretly wiped a perfectly-formed bead of sweat from his scalp (just above his right ear, not that I was paying attention), before removing his hand from his glasses. He didn't take off any of his clothes, not the jacket, not the scarf, not the sweater. No, not he. He was perfectly dressed in the perfect location. In a t-shirt and trousers, sure, but also in a sweater and a jacket and a scarf, there by the sea, in the middle of a hot spring day on the terrace of a hotel, among people watching him drink some orange-colored cocktail, playing with his oversized watch, looking at his phone, fixing his glasses. First with one hand, then with the other. Now he'd wipe a bead of sweat, first with one hand, then with the other.

The women did undress, but not because of the sun. She had undressed because she'd already taken enough selfies while wearing the jacket. She set her jacket down on an empty chair beside her, stretched her long (did I mention that they were very long) legs and slipped them out of those very tall boots. From my vantage, it looked like she was putting on skates, but then I realized it was her actual feet, glossy as if she'd dipped them in wax from heel to toe and had waited for them to harden. Lips fish-puckered, selfies flew forth. She had deeply serious, fleshy dark red lips. As if she'd carefully applied hornet stings that morning.

The man didn't budge. He already knew he was screwed. He was no longer allowed to take off his jacket. If he did, he would reveal to the world a sweat-soaked sweater (maybe that's why it's called a "sweat-er?"). He couldn't afford to let the world see him perspire. So he did the only thing that still seemed a viable option. He loosened his scarf and pushed his shoes off under the table. His reddened face didn't bother him. His audience did not know that he was cooking on the inside. They'd probably think he was just lightly sun kissed.

I couldn't take it anymore. I got up from my chair, made a show of stretching and went back into my room. I couldn't watch this show any longer. I knew too much. It was too painful. I sympathized with him, with all my heart and soul. I knew and understood him. Being and remaining a perfect man is a cornucopia of suffering.

Sexy Lingerie

It would not be inaccurate for me to say that the topic of "sexy lingerie" with my sweetheart was both opened and shut within the first month of our intimate evenings together. Her opinion went something like this: "With erotic undergarments, I shall be even more attractive to my man." To which my implied reply went a little something like this: "Nah."

I never liked lingerie. I'm not sure exactly why not. I guess it always felt like a supplemental obstacle, a frilly, lacy barrier between two people getting to know each other. And for men, those thongs clasping to my butt crack never approached the erotic satisfaction that wearing them promised in those online ads.

One piece of lingerie I've really never liked are those anti-gravitational stockings. The ones that end with a tight silicone strap on the upper half of a women's thigh. They speak to me of hopelessness.

The first time I lay next to my sweety, I was leaning on my left arm. With my right hand, I slowly stroked her hips and ran my finger down her right thigh...and over a swath of silicone tape. My fingers didn't dance over it. I had to press my palm against her thigh to work it past that annoying elastic band. But my palm didn't slide over it, either. It wound up rolling along with my palm into a sort of bunched, twisted coil. I tried to roll it down and away, but it only clomped itself tighter. That silicone tape was stuck in place as if the very Church itself were holding it to keep us chaste.

I couldn't just lie there anymore. I got onto my knees and pulled with sufficient force that the stocking, begrudgingly, rolled off her feet. The maneuver required both hands, but I managed. Then on to the left leg.

She opened her eyes at that moment. She was lying on her back, with her feet in the air, giving me a look. I was still seated next to her, absorbed in my work.

"What are you doing now?"

"I'm sorting your stockings."

What I didn't tell her is that I suffered a sudden wave of nausea, post-traumatic stress from a teenage memory of when I had an early girlfriend beneath me and I thought "Today's the big day." But said early girlfriend said that she was not ready yet.

The action that flashed back this memory was that rolling down motion of textile against skin.

Rolling down with resistance that required both hands.

Rolling down...a condom.

Icarus Dreams

When we boys were still young(er), somewhere around university age, we dreamt of sitting on a plane next to a young, severely sexy babe with perfect teeth (this was exotic in Yugoslavia) and a perfect physique (less exotic). In this fantasy, it was also important to me that she have full lips, that she spoke a lot and liked to laugh. She would allow me to be smart about things I knew and I hoped that she would flash me a sign that she was ready for something more with me. Let's say, for example, that she got up to stretch. She'd slowly step past me, rub her ass around my visage, stand right beside me in the aisle, stretch her arms up to her luggage above my head, so her t-shirt would rise to reveal a perfect belly button. In doing so, she'd notice that I was admiring her physique. She would shyly mention that she was staying at a Holiday Inn (which sounded exotic in Yugoslavia) and that we should probably get together for dinner, because she was sure we had a good connection.

Let it be said that I wasn't exactly a romantic in my youth, so my dreams were a bit more concise than the one outlined above. With age I've embellished the fantasy. At the time, it was more like this: I'm sitting on a plane. Serious babe, full lips, perfect figure, sits in the seat beside me. The plane takes off. She gets up and says she'd like to use the lavatory but isn't sure where it is, and maybe I'd show her? Those airplane facilities can be tricky to locate. We would step into the lavatory together and, like two fecund beasts, get it on. Then we'd return to our seats and never see each other again after landing. That was a key part, in my youth, of course. It had to be crystal clear to my young male brain that we never see each other again. I knew that this would never happen in real life, only in my fantasy realm. My dream would crumble if I'd had any idea that it would actually happen. Impossible imaginary entertainment. The next time I sat next to a babe on a plane, I didn't even dare to look at her or think about cohabiting a lavatory, as I was so afraid that my life partner would read my thoughts.

I first had this fantasy some 25 years ago. Over the last 25 years, I've sat on many a plane, next to people of all races, creeds, weights, odors and lengths of conversation. I sat next to one woman who slept from point A to point B. I sat next to one who looked with terrified eyes out the window every time the plane shook the tiniest bit. But I've never found myself seated next to a severely sexy babe. The boy's dream remains unfulfilled.

I grew up over the years (to some extent, anyway) and stopped fantasizing (so much). Getting on a plane was as commonplace for me as going to the butcher's. I knew everything and each sound was familiar to me. I didn't talk to those seated around me, because I'm bad at smalltalk. Flying has become a boring routine. No fantasies involved. No personal goal.

Until it happened. I was sitting on a plane and a Czech mate sat beside me. A young, severely sexy babe with full lips, perfect teeth and a perfect physique. She laughed easily and was chatty. The babe from my youthful reveries. With one difference. I was now 45 and my dream girl was still 18. She'd only just acquired her driver's license.

I realized quickly that my ship had sailed. My dreams had changed. Now I was dreaming that my dream girl would introduce me to her dream mom.

Too Hot To Hug

It began as innocently as any bloody drama would. Out with friends, we talked about the sleeping habits of our partners. First, a friend recanted a tale of herself and her husband. In it, the lovebirds slept in each other's arms all night long, turning in perfect synchronicity, snoring in tandem, and waking at the same moment. Another couple said that they, too, slept scrunched together in embrace. The third couple, the oldest, slept miles apart. A final, fourth story struck my heart. The quality of that evening's amorous frolic would determine whether the man was permitted to remain through the night sleeping beside the women, or whether she would kick him out and send him home, on a midnight walk of shame.

My girlfriend and I were quiet in the face of these stories. Well, to be perfectly frank, because why not, my girlfriend was also my colleague...that is to say, I was her director. Not that it's important to the story, it's just correct to be open about such things. While these stories were being told, we just mumbled something about needing fresh, cool air to sleep. We invented a cliche (which I quite like): "habit is a matching set of iron pajamas." In short, we avoided explaining our nocturnal arrangement and shifted our attention to the moments before sleepytime, when we would physically manifest our mutual affection, sometimes in multiples. The next day was exhausting and required all of our attention, so we quite forgot about the conversation. That evening we first got to know each other as thoroughly as possible, then we went to sleep.

We did this as we usually do. I was on the right side, closer to the door, so that I could effectively defend my beloved from potential intruders, while my beloved slept closer to the window, so she could be caressed by the first rays of rising sunlight and fresh air that wafted in through the open window. By the time the sunlight reached me, it was somewhat used, second-hand.

That night, we were lying in bed, face to face, our noses touching, but not for long. Soon our heads started to hurt because our eyes were blurry from looking at each other too closely. So we lay in bed, facing each other, but a safe buffer zone of 30 cm separated us. I watched her, my excelsior beauty, her stunning eyes and juicy lips, her exquisite visage, which at the moment looked slightly confused, a bit embarrassed.

"Tell me, my sweet, what's bothering you?"

She smiled at me and whispered. "I'd like to cuddle with you tonight. I'd like to fall asleep in your arms."

My heart fluttered and my eyes misted. I took her hand, kissed her long, slender fingers, stroked her cheeks and nodded. My beauty loves me and wishes to be close, I thought.

"Yes, darling," I whispered back to her. "Let us enthrone our love and fall asleep embracing."

I lay on my left side, stretched my left arm over her pillow, while my angel leaned her head on my biceps, clutched her body to me, leeched her face to my neck, hugged me and I hugged her. My beauty, my queen, her warm, fragrant, long hair. I inhaled that heavenly hair. It smelled wonderful, so I inhaled more deeply. Too deeply. I inadvertently snorted some hair up my nose. Tears welled in my eyes. I did not want to move, to ruin the moment. I loved her and we would fall asleep embracing, as promised. Maybe it would help if I shook my head from side to side a bit? Didn't help. My angel asked me if I was fidgety from sleeping in embrace.

"No, honey," I replied.

With my unpinned hand I stroked her hair and subtly pushed it out of my nostril range. Now it was all good, her hair was at a safe distance from my olfactory organs, and we were hugging warmly. Very warmly, actually. Maybe I was a little hot. In fact, I was very hot. I extricated one of my legs from under the blanket. Not quite enough. Then the other leg.

"Can't sleep?" my doe whispered somewhere along my neck.

"Sure, honey. I'm cooling off a little because you're such a hotty. Good night. It will be a beautiful night. Our night."

My body temperature was somehow still rising. I shifted my legs a centimeter at a time, searching for cold patches of the bed. I inched my back and head up to get a little night air between my skin and the sheets. I'd wiggled my legs so far that they reached the edge of the bed, so I returned them to their original position, like a typewriter at the end of a line. I lifted my boxers up to my balls and slowly shifted my ass outward.

"Can't you be still?"

"Sorry, darling, I'm just a little hot, I'll turn around."

With a soupcon of impatience, she said that I should really go ahead and do so. "So put that arm away," she said, pointing to my left arm which lay pinned beneath her elegant face.

Sadly, I looked at my honey, then at my arm. I took a deep breath, closed my eyes, gritted my teeth and slowly rolled from my left side onto my back. Then I whispered to my dearest: "Uh, I can't move my arm, honey. It fell asleep. Can you just sort of throw it over to me when I turn around?"

I'm Proud Enough To Quit

My beloved has long enforced the idea that I, being a manly man, am meant to blaze trails. I should muck through deep snow to guide others, who cleverly wait for some idiot to walk ahead of them, at which point they'll throw their arms around his shoulders, invite him out for a sausage and wish him happy trails through the snowdrifts.

With this in mind, I sat in a meeting with the very girls in question. The conversation worked its way to the topic of men and women and pain, which women handle better. The argument put forth was the perennial line about enduring childbirth on the women's side, and holding a pot of soup by the handle without using a kitchen towel, on the man's side. Then in swooped the theme of women's self-sacrifice to make themselves more attractive to men, followed by how women do more for men than vice-versa.

At this point I raised my voice in dissent. I am all for equality and mutual respect, I said. I do not see differences among the genders. If I happen to have a kitchen towel to hand, why not fold it four times around the handle of a pot of soup, preventatively of course, while also wearing oven mitts? Wisdom is the mother of the kitchen, I suggested, adding that I had personally sacrificed myself on numerous occasions for the women in my life, even when obliged to endure pain. And, I added nobly, I have bled from my nasal cavities on numerous occasions when trimming my nose hairs with those fucking nail clippers.

They dismissed me with a nonchalant wave of their hands, describing their pain as incomparably more tortuous than mine. Because of my weakness and ego, I then promised that I, as a manly man, a wild, brutal, relentless fist of testosterone, would sacrifice myself for the honor of all men. My version of traversing hot coals would be this: laser hair removal. I would offer up my body to feel what women must go through.

That evening, my sweetheart and I stood before the bathroom mirror. I was nude from the waist up, she sadly was not, and we examined my body, searching for targets that this laser beam could incinerate. The back was a no-go. I don't have much hair there and I do have a tattoo that stretches across my entire shoulder blade. I didn't want changes to my chestal region, and the idea of a laser zapping my nips was too much to bear. What if the laser pierced them? Might I lactate? My legs were a lost cause, as hair has settled there, like a nomadic tribe arriving in the promised land, occupying territory from heel to ass.

Then, my darling eyed her target. She asked me to lift my arms. Reach for the sky.

Oh God, not there, please.

Yes, there. I swallowed hard. My armpits are unusually sensitive. They actually hurt sometimes, though I didn't say this out loud. I chose to suffer in silence, taking one for all my fellow men on this planet. We called the office of Dr. Metka Adamic and, strangely enough, got an appointment...for the next day.

Shit.

Maybe I should just admit that women suffer more for men than we suffer for them?

I weighed the benefits of confession versus a blazing hot laser to the pits.

I chose the laser. It'd hurt less.

It's Not My Fault If She's Dry

I approached my expertise in the kitchen as I did my first joint forays in the bedroom. First, I stood in front of the stove, stared longingly into it, and tried to pull out of my overheated mind everything I'd learned from watching other people do it on TV. I admired the ease of movement of the trained professionals on the screen, how they accessed everything so seamlessly, the performance malleable beneath their fingertips. The man on the screen worked quickly, but elegantly, and he really seemed to enjoy himself. So I decided that I should enjoy it, as well, and set myself the goal. My target: a juicy, perfectly-roasted chick.

I poured hot water to the top of the largest pot. Straight from the fridge I wiped down a hard and chilly chicken. Not to worry, my delightful dining companion, you won't be cold for long. The master will treat you right.

We men understand that you're supposed to soften a bird before you really get into things, so that it does not remain cold and stubborn and tough. I threw all the spices I could find into the pot, hoping at least one of them would take effect.

I cranked up the heat and the water around the bird boiled. Beginning to sweat, I mixed the broth with a long wooden spoon. I turned the bird, so it would be hot on all sides and rubbed the spices into the skin. For a moment the thought struck me that this bird wasn't all that happy with all that spice, but then I rationalized this as not possible. All birds like it spicy, surely. Just in case, I added some more spices that I'd once seen on a show with some other chef.

Delighted, I stirred and turned and the broth boiled so much that I couldn't see the bird for all the spice and foam. I didn't care. It was enough to know that I was fully engaged with her.

In the meantime, my oven had warmed to the appropriate temperature, if you know what I mean. As soon as it seemed that the bird was adequately soft and wet, so juicy that it just wanted finishing, I slid it from the pot onto a roasting pan, added a new round of spices and basted as I've never basted before. Soon, my lovely bird, my crispy one, soon.

The bestial hunger within me was unrelenting. I had to satisfy my urge immediately. I pulled the bird from the oven, my fingers burning as I held her. I placed her, hissing hot, before me and penetrated with my knife.

It was totally dry. How was this possible when I, the chef, had given it my complete well-meaning attention and care, and that she was totally loving every minute of it?

Must've been something wrong with the chicken.

Only One Massage Can Have a Happy Ending

The decision to indulge in a spa massage with my darling was made at precisely 11:10am while we sat on the terrace drinking coffee. Still more precisely, seven minutes later, the reservation was made.

En route to the massage, we considered various ticklish scenarios that might unfold. For example, if presented with a male masseur and female masseuse which of us would get which? If one is a sweet young thing and the other a sweet, well, old thing, which is mine? From the sparkle in my love's eyes I understood that my only viable option was to be thoroughly rubbed by a wrinkled old man, which was diagonally opposite to what nature had programmed me to wish.

We entered the massage room and were instructed to don our thongs. My darling put hers on first. Yes, of course she looked sexy, why do you need to ask? Then I put on my pair. My angel of the morning looked upon me and burst into a spasm of laughter. She couldn't stop. She fell to her knees (good) while staring at my crotch (good) unable to stifle tears of laughter (bad). It wasn't my best look, shall we say. After my painful years of growth and various complexes I finally hoisted myself onto my own two feet. And now this. I found it difficult to accept that my babe was looking at my lion's pride while simultaneously crying and laughing--neither is the reaction you'd hope for when a woman examines your naughty bits. Somehow, midway through her hysteria, she managed to utter the words "Please turn around." As I turned, she fell underneath the massage table, trying to praise my "firm ass" but somehow able only to mutter "aaaaahhhh" between her tears and giggles. I wasn't sure what the problem was. Then I looked in the mirror.

My reflection looked relatively normal, at least to me. Maybe my basket of fruit was a little on the petite side, or maybe I was imagining it. Just then, two masseuses entered the room, radiating experience and sympathy. My love pulled herself together. Neither was too young, too busty or too sexy, so they met with her approval. From my perspective they were both on the positive side of all right, so they met with my approval.

I lay down on my stomach and squished my face into the padded hole thingy for you to put your face in. I was pretty sure that I would only look sufficiently manly if I tensed my muscles, so tense them I did. I imagined that the masseuse would run her hands over them, feel the machismo coursing through me and go mad with desire, lifting me up off the massage table, throwing me against the wall and mounting me with her trained body. Instead, she leaned over and whispered into my ear: "Relax, already. It won't hurt."

My babe and I were being massaged in stereo, on parallel tables. My head was turned towards her, watching as the masseuse slowly slid her oil-slick fingers over my beauty's belly. And I prayed. "Lord, if you exist (pretty sure you do), please make this happen. Just this. Do it for me, for old time's sake. It'd be good for my soul (I'm pretty sure). If you make it happen, then I promise to start believing in you!"

And, lo and behold, she neither massaged my angel's breasts nor reached beneath the thong. Where has the faith gone in this world?

For Once in My Life I'm the Fastest

It happened for the first time when we were in our teens and when time was not our ally. This was most evident during our experiments in intimacy, by which I mean intercourse or, as some people call it, sex. To call it as such, considering the way we did it back then, would be bombastic and aggrandizing, though I will say, hand to, uh, heart that I did the very best I could.

Physically speaking, everything was fine with me. Though, looking in retrospect from the loftier position I hold today, I can say that I was a little impatient in my certainty that I was entering Man Heaven. This conviction confused me, because what I was entering hardly fit this definition of heaven. I imagined that, in heaven, a man can take all the time in the world to perform all manner of mutually consensual acts that the mutual imagination might devise. I have never remained in heaven for anywhere near that long. Because of this, I might even conclude that I was rather entering a very friendly version of Hell.

That day I took a very quick walk to the home of my then girlfriend. Technically, it was her parents' home. Wild with need, I was also pimpled and gaunt. Her parents weren't home, off tending to their own urgent needs or whatever. I didn't know nor did I care. The important thing was that we were alone and coursing with both adrenaline and hormones.

The girl told me to undress and get to work. I did, but it goofed up my concentration because I was wearing a button-down shirt. I thought it would render me more beautiful before God when the heavens opened up to me, but I hadn't counted on the whole having-to-undress thing. It took a fiddly long time to unplug each button from its stranglehold in my shirt. When I finally removed my shirt, I turned around to show my baby my back. "Look what I can do," I said to her, showing off how I could wiggle my shoulder blades, like a pair of pontoons beneath a catamaran, in my skinny body. (This was my idea of foreplay). The show didn't last long.

I quickly realized that I was actually in the room with my willing girlfriend and there I was preparing myself for floating. Yes, I am (make that was) an idiot. We both undressed and finally slipped under the blanket, my eyes shining like the high beams of a car.

"I'm going to prove myself today, I really am," I promised aloud.

I also mentioned that I'd been training my brain all morning, convincing my little grey cells that what we were about to do is actually fun and needn't be categorized as stressful. I then quietly whispered to my upper head that I was in a situation of safety--there were no saber tooth tigers or mammoths around to threaten us, so I was not in need of the fight-or-flight reflex, thank you very much. We were, let's say, lying on a warm cliff with all the time in the world.

As a precautionary measure, I asked the girl to put her t-shirt back on, so as to minimize skin-to-skin contact and reduce the possibility of discovering any new erogenous zones...on me. Then I took her by both hands, just to be certain that she wasn't going anywhere and was not going to ruin my steely concentration. I pulled the blanket towards me and folded it between us, so that we were really not in contact in any but the single most requisite of places. I explain this practical formula to girls, an equation really, that the duration of pleasures is equal to the square centimeter-age between our two bodies divided by the duration of contact. The girl nodded and asked if I could just get on with it, in a way that would be right, of course.

"I trust you," she told me.

I pursed my lips, which quickly drooped down into a shmoo face, angry, wild, with a "nobody messes with me" attitude. Then I inhaled. Then I exhaled. Then I inhaled again. As General, I offered the girl some encouraging commands. These included: "Keep your hands to yourself!" "Don't breathe too much!" "Feet up...wait! Don't move!"

I inhaled again. Then I exhaled again. Three...two...one...now!

I pulled the blanket to the side, jumped on her, entered the gates of paradise. Then the girl moved a bit.

"Stay still! What are you doing!?"

"Sorry."

"Still, still!"

"I'm still."

"Wait! ... Still! Aaaaaaaaaa!"

"Take it out!"

"Too late!"

"What?"

"Stilllllllllllll!"

"Look, I'm completely not moving at all!"

"Noooooooo!"

35 seconds in heaven. I took longer than that to unbutton my shirt.

Next time, when she stops moving around so much, I will totally get close to one minute. A good goal to reach before my thirtieth birthday.

Your Cold is No Obstacle

All week my love and I barely saw each other, so it was no wonder that we could hardly wait for the weekend and its long conversations, late breakfasts and exceedingly hot love sessions (all in reverse order of importance, of course). Truth be told, I could do without the conversations and the breakfasts.

The journey up to our country house atop its hill passed in silence. We arrived, went to the bathroom without saying a word and slipped into our pajamas. I required more time than she did to do so and, by the time I emerged, my darling had already shimmied onto the living room couch and stretched out, feline, beneath a blanket there. This appeared to be several steps in the right direction. I joined her.

All the ideas I'd developed over the past week I planned to implement tonight. I turned on a reading lamp, just strong enough for me to see the outline of the most beautiful face on the planet, the face of my dearest who looked upon me as if I were her demi-god. She didn't just look at me, she ravenously gorged upon me with her eyes. I gorged back. There was no doubt whatsoever--she lusted after me with a barely-contained passion. Her moist, beauteous green eyes glittered like emeralds in the half-light. Her full, slightly open mouth oh-so-discreetly offered the vantage of her perfectly white teeth. She slowly licked her lips and breathed deeply...

I couldn't take it anymore. I sidled up to her, caressed her cheeks, and went in for a kiss, my eyes closed to more fully feel the passionate sense of touch.

Before our lips met, she slipped her hand between us and pushed me away, kicked me off the couch and squawked through her packed nose: "Can't you see that I'm all stuffed up?"

Darn it if I hadn't mistaken the symptoms of passion with the frustratingly similar symptoms of the common head cold. And there I was, about to tear my pants off.

I lay down next to her on the couch. "My dear, shall we roleplay that you watch Farmer Wants a Wife on TV while I approach you from behind and take gratuitous advantage of you?"

She kicked me off the couch again. But I would not be repelled by this curious attempt at foreplay. I climbed back on. "What if we pretend that you're really ill and helpless and I approach you from behind and..."

Then I kicked myself off the couch.

Even Your Proactive Foot Is No Obstacle

My beloved beauty was gently run over by a car. She fell and it kissed her shin. Thankfully, nothing was broken, but she couldn't stand up on her own. The doctor gave her a splint and ordered her to keep her leg elevated.

Living with a loved one who can only move with the aid of crutches, or by pogo-ing on one healthy leg, comes with unique challenges that could be categorized into advantages and disadvantages. When we held hands and frolicked in the park I would normally praise her for her gazelle-like elegance. In doing so, I made it clear that she was slender, youthful, graceful. At the moment, however, she was bouncing like a caffeinated heron. Not that I told her that. I was afraid she would peck my eyes out.

The inherent advantage was that I undressed her more times than usual. I was able to escort her to the shower and gaze upon her as the water cascaded over her magnificent body. I knew that my dear one was struggling, but watching her soap up her radiant skin…while balancing on the slippery tub with one leg while stroking her armpit…well, I couldn't help myself, could I? It was highly entertaining.

But she also had some fun at my expense. When I picked her up and carried her down the stairs, she wrapped her arms around my manly neck, whistled the wedding march in my ear and generally praised me for my manly contributions to her wellbeing. The next time I asked her if she could instead ski down the staircase on her ass.

The good side of having a bum leg is that I always knew where she was. It was wherever I'd last left her. This meant that I could flex my enormous muscles in front of the bathroom mirror without fear of being surprised. And all the other completely normal things that men do when left home alone.

But last night I almost had a heart attack. I was doing something in the kitchen when my beauty wished to shift locations from the couch to the bedroom. Usually this procedure was accomplished by her calling me to move her from the edge of the couch and help her into her splint. Only then could my dove make her way towards her goal.

"Kamenko, where's the splint?"

I sought a clever riposte but, since I couldn't find it, I told her the truth.

"Sorry babe. I have it. You know it's really useful for cracking walnuts. Makes me feel like Iron Man, you know...cool...get it?"

For some reason she didn't find this funny.

Another disadvantage of her multicolored leg was that it had to be raised while she slept. This meant that she covered herself with a blanket over her raised leg, leaving me without a good half of prime real estate blanket. But you shouldn't think that a raised leg was entirely negative. There was also a benefit. As she lay with her right leg raised, I stepped before her, naked as the day I was born. She was uncertain what the heck I was up to, so I calmly explained.

"Look, you have one leg raised anyway because, well, doctor's orders. If you raise the other one that's all I need and half the effort for you."

That night we slept with a splint and a pair of crutches between us.

God of Sex

I sat on a chair at the city's opera house and, for the first time in my life, held an instrument in my hands. A trombone. I pressed the golden horn to my lips and blew.

Nothing. Just an explosion of saliva. I caressed it. Reasoned with it. Blew gently. Raged mightily. Nothing came out of it until the master showed me that sound is produced only when we shake our lips while blowing. Like bumble bees. And our lips must be moist at all times.

All morning long, I licked my lips, snuggled up to the mouthpiece and shook like crazy. The more I shook and the more I licked them, the better that perverse trombone sang. During my first break, my lips trembled so much that I returned the coffee with milk I'd ordered to the waiter because I'd turned it into a cappuccino.

After a whole day of shaking and licking, which some people call "playing trombone in an orchestra," I finally returned home late at night, dead tired. My sweetheart took one look at me and started to paw me delightedly. She's crazy about musicians. She pulled me into the bedroom, pushed me onto the bed and demanded that I kiss her everywhere immediately. Everywhere. With the last ounce of my strength, I played her trombone, extracting a wonderfully sweet sound...and fell asleep.

The next morning I woke up beside her, squeezed against my naked body. She looked at me with admiration and love beaming from her opalescent eyes. She nodded and smiled. She said that she couldn't believe it. That I could do that to her all night. With consistent rhythm. Without pauses. This is something no man before me has been able to do.

I smiled at her, stretched confidently across the bed, licked my lips and, in all humility, permitted her to call me the god of sex.

Buying Gifts? No Thank You

I am a man. A typical man. No better and no worse than your average man. Well, maybe I'm above average in terms of business. And below average in terms of excitement about holidays. Okay, above average in forgetfulness and below average in patience. But that all averages out to being average. And all the average averageness averaged out to shape this year's Valentine's Day.

The issue was made more complex by an incident a few years back, when I failed to meet expectations, in the romance department, for my loved one. To be more precise, I would have easily met, if not exceeded, said expectations had I remembered that there was a holiday to celebrate. I didn't. It drifted past me, like my last car trying to brake over an inch of fresh, powdery snow.

From that point on, my beauty took it upon herself to ensure that I didn't fuck up in this manner in the future. The day before Valentine's, she entered a reminder in my calendar "Buy a gift for Alenka." And another, on Valentine's "Buy a gift for Alenka if you didn't do it yesterday." Good thing she did. That first reminder flashed past me and, on Valentine's Day morning, the most beautiful woman in the world explained in no uncertain terms and with the severity of a serial killer at work that I was not to fuck this up.

She told me she wanted a cosmetic bag and a little bag for lipstick. This struck me as odd. Why would you want one bag to put into another bag? But if she has Russian doll fantasies, why not. Oligarchs with a big yacht like to have a smaller yacht parked inside it, right?

On Valentine's morn, I stood in front of a shop, alongside a lineup of other men, with a blank, sheep-like gaze, waiting for it to open. I took a deep breath and, armed with instructions from my darling, stepped into the abyss.

I walked slowly around the store, the saleswomen trailing me with their eyes, smiling and flirting. There were an unusually large number of them. One next to each bottle of shampoo, as I recall. I walked an imaginary line that was equidistant from the saleswomen to my let and right. I was hoping that they would leave me alone. This tactic proved unsuccessful.

"Hello, how can I help you?" A cute, dark-haired woman surprised me with a rear attack.

"No need, thank you," I replied, aiming my words at the floor so I wouldn't have to look her in the eyes, because they were of course beautiful eyes and of course perfectly made-up and that would bury me. "I learned to walk forty-four years ago, so I'm good."

I was looking for a shelf containing handbags, but they weren't among the cosmetics. That would be the most logical place to keep them, but male logic doesn't hold water in a store of this nature. If you ask a man, he'd tell you that a bag for cosmetics should be displayed somewhere between the cosmetics and the bags. Or maybe, at a stretch, in the textile department, since it's made of, I guess, textiles? Nope. The cosmetic bags were hidden behind a shelf full of jewelry. This was clearly designed to make men look silly as they wander around the store, and to encourage saleswomen to come and rescue them.

"Can I help you now?"

"Yes please," I surrendered, stammering. "Handbags, small, large, one inside the other, pretty..."

The lady with the big, beautiful eyes escorted me to the proper shelf, which contained millions of eyeshadows of all tints and shapes.

"What color would the lady want?" she chirped as she stood so close that I inhaled her perfume. I noticed her perfectly white teeth. She was tall and wore tight black trousers and a tight black shirt. Lord have mercy. My muffin was baked.

Luckily, we men of maturity have experience on our side. Once, long ago, I accidentally heard my love mention a color.

"Purple" I blurted out.

My hands began to sweat. The saleswoman approached the shelf, stretched out her hand, and brushed against my biceps with her chest. I stopped breathing.

"Sir, is this one okay?"

In her hand she held a purple purse with white dots. No, two of them, one smaller and one larger! I took a deep breath. Five Euros and Nine Euros? That was too little. I would have to buy something else to go with it. My expression clearly indicated panic and the need for assistance.

"How else can I help you?"

Now I gathered myself and said, confidently, "I would also like a cream, a quality cream, for women."

She took me by my arm to the other end of the store. There stood two saleswomen waiting for me with such broad smiles that I forgot to check out their physiques.

"What price range are you interested in, sir?"

"Only the quality is important," I replied presumptuously, realizing that I had screwed myself over the moment the sounds emerged from my lips. The Three Graces smiled back to me, their grins stretching all the way to the Black Sea, as they positioned me in front of a shelf of creams, pulled my sleeves up both arms, and smeared me lengthwise and crosswise with testers.

My darling was delighted with the handbags. The right colors and sizes. She hugged me, snuggled me, kissed me. I stroked her hair with my velvety soft male hand, which had been nurtured with a gift I indulged in for myself that holiday--a hand cream with a pleasant texture and a reassuringly high panthenol content that protected my masculine skin and strengthened my manly nails.

I Can't Get Drunk

My sweetheart and I required two days to settle into our main annual holiday on the seaside. Let me clarify: our holiday came down to fifteen meters. Not in square meterage. Rather I mean that it was precisely fifteen meters from our room to the food and fifteen meters from the food to the ocean. On the beach we had sun fifteen meters to our left and shade fifteen to our right. It was fifteen meters from where our car was parked to our room. Our adventurous holiday-making moved in precisely fifteen meter increments, which turned out to be just the right spacing for a vacation full of incidents great and small.

A life in which food is only fifteen meters away has its pros and cons. Witness the following pro and con: the food in the hotel restaurant was so good that, right after lunch, my beauty asked aloud "Yum, what's for dinner?" Whenever we left the beach, we told the waiters our desires regarding food and drink, we ran up to our room, showered, and came downstairs. There would be a table with drinks waiting for us, the food to arrive shortly after we were seated. What could be a con in this situation, you may ask? Well, we did want to explore the delights of the seaside town in which we holidayed. That meant that, every time we walked past the hotel restaurant and didn't want to eat in it, we felt the traitorous pangs of guilt. We flipped through various excuses to make to the wonderful hotel staff.

"Today is our trip into town," we once said.

On another day, we tried, "We're out of fruit, we're running to the market."

And then, "Today we're not really hungry, we ate so much for lunch."

Yeah, none of that sounded convincing to me, either. We quickly ran out of excuses and ate all our meals, consumed all our coffee, indulged in all our desserts in the hotel restaurant. Knowing we didn't dare go anywhere else after dinner, I ordered a beer to go with my main course and poured it directly into myself. I sipped a second beer during dessert and came perilously close to giggling and snorting like a child.

We were almost through our semifreddo when one of the waiters approached and proudly offered us glasses of sweet moscato wine, compliments of the hotel. It was a kind gesture from our hosts, so we thanked them from the bottom of our hearts, without confounding them with the detail that my darling doesn't like white wine. Glasses in hand, we sat down at a table by the beach and smiled and nodded to the waiter, who was constantly watching us indulge in the treat he'd brought. His colleagues eyed us, too. All of them, actually. Pendulous guilt swung in the sea air. We were going to have to drink this wine, one way or another.

My dearest made it clear to me that she had suffered headaches every time she'd ever consumed white wine, and that I was on my own, when it came to imbibing. I already was two beers to the wind and knew I was at my limit. But at no cost could my beloved have a headache that evening. Fortunately, I was born with innate improvisational skills. My plan was bold and clever. I engaged my darling in an overtly humorous conversation, during which we touched, laughed, teased aloud, and otherwise distracted attention from what was happening on the table beside us. Without anyone noticing, I placed both glasses in the center of the table, side by side, and turned them like I was playing Three Card Monte. Then I waited for the waiter to look at me. I grabbed a glass, raised it to greet him, and took a big sip. He nodded contentedly, and devoted himself to other tasks, while I swapped locations of the glass. A little later, when the waiter looked over again, I took another hearty sip but now from the other glass, before I put it back on the table and rotated to the first glass. In under twenty minutes I'd spun my way into drinking both glasses of wine. We asked for the bill and headed off to our room, taking the stairs gingerly.

My babe was the first to hit the shower. Then it was my turn. But by the time I was back in our bedroom, she was sound asleep.

That had not been our agreement. I sacrificed my own body so she wouldn't have a headache, so we could cap our evening in a sort of a victory dance, and now this? My head was spinning. I had to let her know how I felt, that I deserved her attention.

In mock-awkwardness I kicked the bed. My darling awoke, lifted her head and looked at me.

"What are you doing?"

I lay down beside her on the bed. I bent my knees and pulled them to my chin. For a time, I stared at her blankly. I finally managed to open my mouth but all I could say before I fell asleep was, "Sorry, sweetheart. I know you wanted me to rock your world, but I'm afraid it's bedtime..."

She's Gonna Bury Me

On the last morning of our holiday, over a sumptuous breakfast, my beauteous one got the bright idea to make homemade jam, and so planned to buy a whole mess of apricots at the stall near the hotel.

We sat in the car in front of the hotel, and my babe told me to drive towards the stand. I replied that there was nowhere to park near the stand and it was not far at all and shouldn't we really go on foot. She rolled her eyes and made it clear that this ridiculous suggestion was not an option. I replied with wit and grace by slamming the car door shut and driving out of the parking lot. We stopped fifty yards later, in the middle of an intersection, because we couldn't move further.

"See where you're taking us now?"

"Leave the car here and you can walk to the stall."

Bravo, Madam, a clockwork plan.

Oops. It appeared that Madam was serious.

Naturally I left the car parked in the middle of the intersection. I huffed it the remaining yardage to the stand, arriving red from heat and exertion.

"20 kilos of apricots, please!"

"25 kuna."

I gave him a 100.

"Do you have anything smaller?"

I have a smaller annoyance sitting back there in the car, awaiting my return. I brought the apricots, which my mood had lightly steamed, to the car and threw them in the trunk. We drove home in silence.

"Sorry I was annoying," she whispered to me after a while.

"Sorry I was grumpy," I replied.

"I just want to be yours. Forever."

"I also want to be just yours. Forever."

"Will we be together for the rest of our lives?"

"We will, my darling."

"Am I the last woman in your life?"

"Yes, darling."

It took me a few moments to understand what had just happened to me. I saw my destiny spread before me. Beside me sat the woman who would bury me.

PART TWO

Marriage

Tiffany is Late with a Ring

It all began two months ago. I ordered an engagement ring online from a branch of the Tiffany jeweler in London. A cute-sounding saleswoman was my accomplice. She understood my wishes, we spoke on the phone a few times and we had plenty of time to process the order and send me the ring in time for showtime.

Two weeks later, I heard not a word about the ring. The saleswoman calmed me down. "Sir, I've got you covered. Everything is under control."

I understood. Everything was under control. I left it to the experienced salespeople and consultants. Every now and then I sent an email anyway. How was it going? Any progress?

"Sir, everything is as it should be. I've got you covered. Don't worry about a thing."

The week before leaving for Vienna, where I planned to propose, no one at the London Tiffany branch knew where my ring was. My Booking.com reservation page was open on my computer constantly, with my cursor hovering over the "CANCEL RESERVATION" button. Five days before we were to leave, the saleswoman called me.

"Sir, we have solved the mystery of the missing ring. You are now safely in my hands. Not to worry."

Not to worry? I closed all the doors and windows of the house. I stepped into the middle of the living room and released the loudest, wildest, most bestial primal scream I could muster.

A moment later, I sent the entire itinerary of our Vienna trip to London and gave them free rein as to where they could find me to get me that ring en route from Ljubljana to our hotel in Vienna. At the entrance to the hotel room, even, secretly slipping me the ring in a gloved palm, espionage film-style.

The day before we left, a different salesperson took over my case.

My guardian angel had, apparently, gone on a doubtless well-deserved vacation.

I missed the deadline to cancel my reservation. My darling was delighted to be taken to Vienna. I told her I needed to unplug as I'd had it up to here with everything. That was really the case. I just didn't specify to her to which "everything" I referred.

On the day of our departure, I sat in my office and came to terms with my fate. Apparently there would be no proposal on this trip. I muttered obscenities under my breath, directed indirectly at all the employees of all branches of this storied jeweler, the world over. Then I calmed down, threw my laptop into my backpack, told my dearest to be ready in thirty minutes, and I bid my colleagues farewell.

"Kamenko, something just came for you," said the guy at the front desk, pointing to a small box. I once more muttered obscenities, but now just preventatively. I grabbed the box, carefully slipped it into my backpack and headed for the car.

Question-Popping

After a few hours, we stepped into the extravagant lobby of the Ritz-Carlton Hotel. Every one of the employees I spotted had earbuds in their ears. We were assigned a room number at the front desk, the receptionist pressed a button that was hidden beneath her shirt and whispered something into it. The suitcases set off on pilgrimage to our room (requiring a 10 EUR tip) and the car was taken to the garage (40 EUR per day).

At the front desk, we were offered hot, damp towels with which to wipe our hands and a man dressed as a butler escorted us to the room. I'd booked a room on the top floor of the hotel. The penthouse: sufficiently chic for such an occasion. It was clear to me what I needed to do. Step into the room. Take her hand. Turn her towards me. Kneel. Pop open the box and say "Alenka, you turned my world upside-down...etcetera, etcetera." I'd memorized my speech (which didn't actually include the word "etcetera"). I'd repeated it countless times, to myself and out loud. The butler opened the door for us. My darling stepped into the room and started to shout with delight, "Check this out! They have a Nespresso machine! Look at the tea selection! The room is so big! And champagne..."

This all made me dizzy. The price of the ring, the price of the hotel, the price of the dinner to come. I responded in the only way I could.

"Careful not to accidentally open the champagne or I'll go bankrupt!"

"But it's gotta be free if they just left it out on the table."

My stare in response could have sliced bread.

My primary concern at that moment was one of logistics. We were both standing in the room, so there was no way to extract the ring inconspicuously. Thankfully, my dearest rushed to my aid.

"I've gotta pee. I'm guessing they've got the coolest bathroom ever."

Go, my dove, and scream with delight behind the closed door of the bathroom to your heart's content.

She closed the bathroom door. I heard a squeal of joy. I reached for my backpack and slipped the box containing the ring under my pillow. Now I just had to wait for her to emerge and the romance could commence.

It was unusually quiet in the bathroom. Had she fainted? If so, I still had time to get my hair done.

"Kamenko," I finally heard her call.

"What is it, my dove?"

"There's no brush." She sounded worried.

"What brush? A hairbrush?"

"They don't have a brush to...clean with."

Huh?

I took a deep breath. Now was the time to keep my cool.

"Alenka, they don't leave out brushes in hotels like this. It's not your job to clean..."

We spoke from either side of the bathroom door.

"Okay, but what if, hypothetically, one of us has to go Number Two? How are we supposed to brush the toilet bowl?"

Ah, I understood a bit more. "Honey, others will clean up after us," I continued calmly.

"Are you nuts!? No way in Hell is anyone cleaning my Number Two!"

I stood in the middle of the most expensive and beautiful hotel room in Vienna and stared at the pillow under which waited our engagement ring. I'd never imagined that I would be debating about excrement just before popping the question. About poop before the pop, as it were.

"Honey, it's that kind of hotel. Forget about it, please," I continued, impatient.

"Not on your life. I'll find a way to erase the traces of my Number Two," she sharply retorted.

"What do you care if someone else cleans up after you, dammit! Come out already!"

"You think it's all the same to you, but then you go down to breakfast and all the staff look at you because they know you were pooping and leaving a dirty bowl!"

Geez Louise, this is the woman I'm going to marry? What will she get me for a wedding gift? A toilet brush?

"Come on, come on out...we'll talk about it." It was my last attempt before I blew my top.

The bathroom door finally opened.

"I'm going to slip into some slippers," she said.

What's next? How about we head to the gym? Maybe the hairdresser?

"Come, hold your horses. Let's just sit on the bed for a moment, please."

She looked at me, confused, and sat down on the bed. I knelt in front of her. I could see on her face that she'd figured out what I was up to. I reached under the pillow, popped open the box and showed her the most beautiful ring of our lives, shining before us. Tears ran down her cheeks.

"Alenka," I began.

She sat there, watching me and waiting. I couldn't say a word more. I'd forgotten the whole speech. Everything I'd been repeating and practicing the last month. A curse upon all the Number Twos and toilet brushes of this world!

Eight Weeks Til Showtime

I was sitting on the terrace of my house, on a hill eight-hundred meters above sea level. Alone on a lounger, the sun at my back. My sweetheart flitted about tending to the household, as did the bees that hummed about my ears. A cuckoo in the forest cuckooed like a cuckoo. It was as if I were living inside my father's wall clock, with some 1030 minutes ticked away.

I would be married in eight weeks. For the second time. My betrothed would also be marrying for the second time. I am two months older than she is. We've both been divorced for six years. We each have two children from a previous marriage. In eight weeks we tie the knot.

My wife-to-be is a real woman. Based on this statement I conclude that I, therefore, must be a real man. I am 46 years old, healthy, physically fit, 191 cm tall (6'2") and weigh in at 98 kilos (215 lbs). My hair is black and my complexion is a Mediterranean-Balkan burnished olive. I am satisfied in business and happy in life. Our children are healthy. We both get along very well with our exes. Do I have a life motto? I do. Mene ne bo noben jebo. How do I translate this? The most direct way is: "Nobody screws with me." Even when it comes to marriage.

It was all crystal clear. I'd read enough online articles on what a man should devote his attentions to before, during and after a wedding. I'd imbibed the opinions of the minority of writers who claim that it's difficult to get along in marriage. I say unto them, "Ha!" Or those who say that a wife should be the only one who offers carnal pleasures to her husband. "Ha!" Hang on, yes of course that's correct.

Bottom line: I was ready for a wedding much as any real man prepares for any big event. Almost.

If it were up to me, on a predetermined Saturday I would bedeck myself in the handsomest garb in my closet, stroll over to the registry office at the town hall, exhale the words "I do," treat myself to lunch and then head back home to mow the lawn and prepare a barbecue for friends and family that evening. If it were up to me.

It wasn't up to me.

At home, in the closet, I have a very comfortable, elegant pair of black shoes. Comfortable, to a real man (which I am) means nicely worn in after many years of stalwart use and with a design that, wouldn't you know it, is back in fashion again. These were particularly fresh-looking because I'd recently taken them to a renowned cobbler for, well, refreshing. They looked like new.

Alas, my dearest had determined that they were insufficient for the purpose of standing in front of an altar.

But you know me, I didn't complain (much) about the rejection of my favorite shoes. Buying a new pair would be easy-peasy. I'd browse online stores which would offer a good enough discount mixed with good enough quality to have me sorted in no time.

After a few days of browsing, I completed Phase One of this project. I ordered six pairs of shoes, each priced around 150 EUR but around 50% off and all with the option of a return and full refund. Most were black, Oxford style. Some were brown because I liked them. Nothing easier than dressing for a wedding.

She didn't like the first pair to arrive by post. Too shiny.

The second pair was ugly.

The third was beautiful, but not suitable for a wedding, seeing as they were brown.

The fourth and fifth pairs were a bit too tight.

The sixth looked different than it had in the photo.

All six packages were shipped back from whence they came. No need to panic, we still had plenty of time. I shimmied back online again, ordered three new pairs, this time priced at around 300 each (though, of course, discounted by half).

I sent all three pairs back, for one reason or another. And so it was with a third and fourth batch of shoes.

Time to panic?

After two months of ordering, testing and returning shoes, the cost of return postage approached the amount I was willing to spend on shoes in the first place. And I still had exactly no new shoes. If I were to buy everything on my (strike that: Alenka's) wish list using the same strategy I'd employed for shoes, then I'd be getting married in gray trousers to match my gray hair and the silvery glint of my cane.

A real man knows when to take drastic measures. Action was called for. And that action had to be swift, well-considered and risk-free.

I first consulted with the future Mrs. Kesar. I asked her to describe how she imagines me at the wedding. "I imagine George Clooney."

I imagined I didn't hear her say that.

"What about at least Ryan Gosling?" It was harder to imagine I didn't hear two statements in a row, but I did my best. She continued, specifying "George and Ryan are both wearing nice, black tuxedos."

The advice of the future queen of my castle put things into perspective.

As for the shoes, a solution volunteered itself. It had to be a top drawer purchase since it had to fit with a tuxedo. And there was no time to get the sizing wrong. No risk, alas, meant no discounts.

So it was: Allen Edmonds. Plain toe. Size 11.5. Width E.

As for the tuxedo, I turned to the only online store where I knew I could buy a wedding suit that would look like I'd been poured into it. The German emporium Herrenausstatter.

Without risk, alas without discount to speak of. Neither the tux nor the shoes were pompous, they fit me perfectly and they were neatly tucked away in the closet to await showtime.

That evening in bed, I boasted to my beloved that I'd sorted out both tux and shoes, even if I'd had to pay full price. She held her breath for a moment then rolled her eyes like an impatient teenager.

"Two months ago if you'd asked my opinion you would've arrived at the same solution sooner and cheaper." She finished her scolding with the punctuation of turning away from me. Perhaps my love was correct? But before I'd decided to follow her advance, I also bought a dress shirt, socks, a tie and a pocket square. As real men know all too well, asking your spouse and then buying everything correctly the first time around is just plain boring.

Blame the Barber

I stood in front of her and watched as my beloved stared at me. The silence was eloquent. She didn't like what she saw. Before she could say anything, I leapt in, like a real man in a hopeless situation.

"Frank suggested that we test it out."

Frank, or rather Franck (forgive him, he's French), as he liked to spell it, was my hairdresser. That's what you call a very expensive barber at a very expensive hair salon on one of the very expensive streets in my not very expensive hometown. It ain't cheap, but it's the only place that knows how to trim the tufts atop my pumpkin, if you know what I mean. And I can talk to Fran(c)k about anything. Really anything. He doesn't judge, he just gives his opinion and we move on to the next topic. He also shared my desire to cut my hair in time for our wedding. The order was clear and decisive.

"Frank, give me the shortest thing you've got, but make sure that it's good enough that you'll want to sign your name prominently beside your creation."

This didn't strike him as correct. He told me this, bringing the only voice of reason into this story by posing a logical question.

"Do you have the permission of your future bride?"

Permission? I most certainly did not, Fran(c)k, goddamn buttery croissant, why do you even ask? Make it short because short is how I have the least work with my hair in the morning. And while you're cutting, help me cook up a story about why it's short to sell to my future bride that will allow me to sound smart and visionary.

He found one. A story, I mean. It sounded magical, clever, ingenious...a wow. I could hardly wait for my beauty to cast her eyes upon me and for me to explain Frank's super plan to her.

I stood before her as she watched me.

"What did he SUGGEST? What TEST?" Are you CRAZY? WHAT IS

THIS?" (She actually spoke in CAPS as she pointed to my pumpkin.)

I took a deep breath and thought to myself that my dearest just didn't recognize true genius at work, even when it was tufted right before her eyes. I exhaled Frank's story:

"Look, Frank said that we should go very short so that I can witness how my hair grows. When my hair is just the right length for the wedding, I can then calculate how many days it's been since the haircut, and I can call and tell him. This way we can reproduce that perfect hair length for the wedding, by getting it cut the precisely correct number of days before the wedding."

That night we did not make love.

The next day, Alenka's friends came by for a visit. Adult, poised, intelligent, real women. Women of culture who should recognize the genius of the hairdressing test and congratulate me on it. They should hug me, turn to my beloved and compliment her on having chosen such a smart future husband.

As they sat down in the living room, I stepped before them and presented myself. They simultaneously cast their eyes to the floor and remained silent, destroying me without words. Oh, Fran(c)k, why did you do it?

Fighting Against Costs at All Costs

Six weeks before the wedding there was no time to panic. Hang on, let me adjust that. Six weeks before the wedding, there was time to panic every waking second. There was no time to panic because there was so much panicking.

Correspondence with the hotel catering manager, on the subject of catering, was conducted in calm tones. No one had the energy for berating. Not the hotel manager, who had a new wedding to handle every week and was on the edge of sanity because of this, and not I, for I had another six weeks on the edge of sanity for other reasons.

Alenka and I had organized our wedding to take place in the beautiful town of Opatija, on the Croatian coast, in the elegant Hotel Kvarner. The catering manager, preferably referred to with the more refined title of F&B manager (food & beverage--I had to look it up, too), was the one responsible for two of the three most important things to our wedding at this hotel. You guessed it: food and beverage. I was responsible for the most important thing. My heart, my love, my dearest...in all senses of the word "dear." Yes, I was responsible for paying the wedding expenses. In this spirit, we had a sophisticated and quality-based email correspondence regarding the choice of food and drink.

"Hi, I'd like to have cocktails at midnight."

"Dear Sir, one cocktail per person will cost five euros."

"Hi, thank you. Too expensive. Please send me a chemical analysis of your tap water and the price of bottled water, if the analysis appears overly-toxic."

Alas, it was not easy to negotiate a lower price with the hotel. My approach was clearly insufficiently sophisticated. Fortunately, my brilliance knew no end. I hit upon an idea of how to save money on liquid intoxicants.

"Hi, in consultation with the wedding band, we've agreed on an alcohol-free party."

"Dear Sir, hahahahahahahahahahaha."

I started thinking that it might be easier to save on food...perhaps instead, perhaps as well.

"Dear Sir, we can serve a nice soup around 2am."

"Hi. How much do I save if I ladle out the soup myself?"

Or:

"Dear Sir, for a cold appetizer we can serve king prawns on a bed of arugula."

"Hi, might it be possible, at the same price, of course, to serve a leaf of arugula on a bed of king prawns?"

"Dear Sir, of course. The price of the prawns remains the same."

They did not allow me to funk up their groove. Not yet, at least. They didn't realize they were dealing with a professional groove funker. I am a pro problem-solver. Even those that appear insurmountable.

After a few days in deep thought, perusing the contract, I found a loophole. Children aged 0-3 ate and drank for free!

From that point on, I had the costs under control. It wasn't easy, but I managed to swap out the majority of our friends and family for random parents with preschoolers.

The Honeymoon that Involved Neither Honey nor the Moon

Five weeks before the wedding, we took a break from marriage planning. Off we went on a short holiday to Barcelona, to attend a pair of long-awaited concerts: Adele and Coldplay. I tried to sell this to my darling as a honeymoon, but before I had actually said as much, just after I'd uttered the words, "You know, my beauty, I was thinking...," she stopped me with an overly-enthusiastic squeeze of her fingers into my jugular, then pulling her face a nose away from mine and hissing, "Really, Kesar? You're thinking!? Don't you know that thinking is not in your best interest?"

Yup, that's why I love her. We have such richly engaged debates.

Honeymoons before the wedding. Has that, like, ever happened? I smiled through my spasm and managed to grunt, "Of course...my tigress...please...release...my...neck."

The plane ride to Barcelona would've been nothing special, but my lovely lady is afraid of flying. We'd flown together several times and she always took my hand. And clenched it until both hers and mine were white. This time was different. My babe nuzzled close to me, scrunched into my neck, trying to hide her entire body behind my right ear, and waited for the terror to pass.

I understood. After all, we'd be wed soon. Who besides me should comfort her? In this situation, on a plane, I could only offer a slow and gentle stroking of the hair form of comfort. She liked it. She repaid my largesse with a kiss on my neck and ear. I comforted her a little more with the hair stroking thing. And she repaid me again. Somewhere over the Austrian Alps, something started happening to me. Only to me. And it didn't stop until we landed in Barcelona. The plane pulled to a halt, my sweetheart dropped my bloodless hand from her death grip and peeled her face off of my neck. I looked at her like a stunned wombat. How could I not? She had uncovered a brand new erogenous zone on my body, one I'd never known about.

Despite the careful planning of the aforementioned journey, i.e. the plane reservation, the hotel and tickets to two concerts, we were fully surprised on the first evening. It all began at the hotel reception.

"We're hungry," we said, followed by "tapas would..." A friendly receptionist fiddled with the computer and looked for a good local tapas place. She then asked colleagues and checked on Tripadvisor. She chose a place for us and marked its location on a map. She calculated the cost of the taxi, printed out a sheet of information about the restaurant, added her own recommendation on what to order and called the taxi for us. She opened the door of the taxi on our behalf and wished us bon appetit and smiled, having proudly made someone's evening better, before she returned to her place of work. We, on the other hand, sat in a taxi with the address of the restaurant on a printout, proud as a pair of roosters, hungry as a pair of dogs, impatient as a pair of penguins in front of the closed freezer door.

The friendly taxi driver was informed where we were headed. I pushed the printout into his hands. It read Cerveceria Catalana. He nodded, "Okay, we locals ate there, too, but not anymore, because there are too many tourists." Off we drove.

A mile further on, and we were fast friends with the driver. My darling launched into the topic of football and said that she was a little disappointed that it was the end of the season and there was no match for us to attend. "Yeah, you came at the wrong time," the driver said, salting our wounds. You couldn't even attend training sessions during this period. "A shame you'll have to leave without having this beautiful experience."

He abruptly fell silent and turned on the radio. Then he turned to us. "But...but today...they just said...I completely forgot...today is free....," he could barely breathe with excitement, "today is the celebration of the Double Crown...free."

My dove and I locked eyes. Even the taxi driver locked eyes with us, ignoring the road as it sped before him. Someone would have to make an executive decision if, for no other reason, simply to avoid a collision.

"To the stadium!" I shouted. "Floor it, man!"

The driver shouted, "Yeah! That's how it's done!" The tires squealed, other drivers pounded on their horns. A rush of adrenaline filled the car. My darling mentioned dinner, but it was quickly agreed that we could have dinner later and elsewhere, who cared about being hungry or about the best tapas in town?

After a few minutes, we arrived at the stadium entrance. We leapt out of the taxi and rushed to the first scalper we could find selling the "free" tickets. I pushed ten Euros into his hand so we didn't have to find a ticket booth. We ran into the stadium, bought three giant hot dogs and a Coke and sat in our seats. We leaned back, hugged and admired, with a smile, the beauty of Barcelona, the fireworks and Iniesta, who the whole stadium deified. I glanced at my beauty by my side. My own goddess. We would soon be married. She noted my look and leaned over to me. "Tomorrow we're going to the beach. I'll quickly soak in the sun. A little color would do me good. I'll be a more beautiful bride." I nodded.

We went to the beach in the morning. Everywhere I looked I saw bleach-white Englishmen lying in the sun. Two hours later, they resembled Lobster Thermidor. I wasn't sure whether to call them an ambulance and approach with a two-pronged fork and a bowl of melted butter. My angel and I were dismayed at this behavior. Wasn't it clear to them that this was not dermatologically recommended? Didn't they remember the previous holiday when they came away just as badly burned? Didn't they notice, for example, us, remaining under a parasol at all times? We just braved the sun to stand in line in front of the restroom at the beach. Or when we went for ice cream. Or a coffee. Or two coffees.

Sometimes even when we were chilled to the bones in the shade and we briefly fell asleep, we'd step into the sun to promote the renewed circulation of our venal system. We were very careful to remain in the shade. British Islanders are clearly missing the part of the brain that relates to the union of logic and tanning.

That evening we stood in our hotel room. We couldn't undress. We couldn't lie down. We couldn't sleep at all. Despite all our precautions, we still were sunburned.

Honey, I've Found the Wedding Rings

A month before the wedding, the day after returning from Barcelona, my beloved and I took a day off. We planned to drive down to Opatija. She was supposed to arrange the documents with the registry office there. The registry office website declared that it would be open until 4pm. Since that gave us all morning, we decided to pop over to Zagreb, the Croatian capital, first. There, in a jewelry store in the city center, wedding rings awaited us. They'd been ordered online a few weeks prior. I didn't expect any particular drama there. We stepped inside, gave them our names and added that we'd come for "those" rings. The saleswoman perked up disconcertedly. "Yes, I have them, they are here, they are definitely here, right away," she sang happily. She stepped behind the counter, pulled out a box, placed it before us and opened it.

Two beautiful rings lit up before our eyes. Exactly what we wanted. We put them on. We were satisfied. So was the saleswoman, apparently. "I have something to tell you," she said, mysteriously. "You were the first to order these rings. Ever. No one before. Everyone else thought they were weird."

My future bride and I exchanged looks. We weren't sure just what to do with this statement. If this had happened in a restaurant, the waiter confiding "You're the first people to ever order this dish, everyone else thought it was too weird," I would have fled the establishment. At a jewelry store? Thinking pragmatically, the three of us agreed that this is probably a good thing, and the conversation shifted to more traditional topics, like the wedding, family and, especially, men...

"What happens to them after forty?" the saleswoman suddenly asked my bride-to-be, as if I was not there. "I come home dead tired from work, I cook, I wash, I tidy up, I feed the baby, I cuddle him a little, and when I throw myself down on the couch, my husband looks at me as if he's been starving for a week and asks 'What about me?' Doesn't he understand that I need peace? Do I have to take care of two children or what?"

Feeling pale of face and petrified of legs, I tried to make myself even paler and more sculptural. If the saleswoman shifted one gear more into rage, I was directly in the line of potential fire. My darling looked at her sympathetically and gave her opinion in a soft voice, speaking of the needs of men, of the second puberty that comes in middle age, about sex and attention. She spoke right through me, as if I weren't there.

So I stood in the jewelry store for nearly ten minutes, not being there, not daring to move (and call attention to my continued presence) to interrupt an honest conversation between two women about their men, unfolding before my eyes. I wanted to raise my hand and say, "Yo, man in the room!" But this I deemed unwise. I waited for them to say what they needed to say. For example, my dear lovingly and with deep understanding explained that the saleswoman must not forget that, for her husband, she is first and foremost a woman, a mistress, and that she must find chemistry between them if she wants her husband to be happy and satisfied.

When she said this, the saleswoman walked past me and hugged my beloved. "I've never hugged a customer in my life," she said. "Thank you. Thank you."

We took to the street. I stopped and looked at my betrothed.

"What was that?"

"Life, my love, life. Welcome."

We missed the registry office, which was open until 4, by 20 minutes. Because they worked until 3.

Accommodating the Relatives

It is three weeks before our nuptials and my days are filled with meeting of known and less known relations, with many pats-on-the-back and smiling thumbs-ups.

"Three more weeks, isn't that right?"

This comment is meant to convey that they've read my blog, that they sympathize and, as in The Truman Show, they've been virtually riding shotgun along every step of my life as a single gentleman, a life that will swiftly be extinguished and reborn into, well, something else. There were still a few weeks before the wedding and so much more to do that my darling and I wondered if we'd be able to handle it all. But I, manly man that I am, wasn't panicking. There would be food. There would be music. There would be beverages. There will be a ballroom, containing at least four walls, a floor and a ceiling, in which said activities will be made available. What could possibly go wrong?

"Sir, you know that the ballroom you've booked…how shall I put this…it's equipped only with white lights, no colors, no liveliness." That was the opening line used by the hotel-recommended decorator to kick off what I call The Buying Show. He sold us multicolored LED spotlights which "are tucked away behind a curtain and create a feeling of warmth in the ballroom if it's cold outside, and of course the opposite if it's warm outside."

The head of protocol from the hotel assured us, behind the decorator's back, that we don't need any extra light in the ballroom because we could regulate the intensity of the lights already installed, which are already so strong that they could induce temporary blindness if used at maximum capacity. We were happy to convey this information to the decorator.

"Okay," he replied, "just as long as you won't regret it later. Let's leave it at that, but instead, for just a small fee, you can at least get your chairs covered in fabric. The ones the hotel provides for free are really not up to snuff."

It wasn't clear to me why the decorator was slandering the very hotel that employed him. But who am I to judge? It was up to me to pivot the situation to my advantage and extract maximum value for minimum expenditure. I called the head of protocol again.

"I hear you give out chair covers for free, but I see that there's a charge for them in the quote. Are we going to have a problem?"

"We won't have a problem," he replied, "we'll give you the chair covers for free, candlesticks for free, half-price on drinks for kids, and we'll tie ribbons around the white chairs at no extra charge." I enjoy triangular negotiations.

Yesterday, the love of my life and I lay upon the couch for the first time since our return from Barcelona. We were both lightly toasted, our backs no longer hellishly scorched. We considered the important step before us. I stroked her hair and inhaled deeply the scent of her neck.

"Did you double check the room reservations for the relatives?" she suddenly asked.

I didn't, my dove, nor does it occur to me to do so now that I've passed Steps One and Two of foreplay, in rapt anticipation of Steps Three through Seven. Alas, the bride to be was not ready to shift topics so easily. She made it clear that I could easily retread Steps One (fingers stroking hair) and Two (neck sniffing) later. Now onto more important work. I flatlined my lips, stood abruptly and breathed deeply. I then kicked a slipper so it skittered across the floor. This was in order to make it clear that the reservation checking could have really waited another two minutes, which was all I really needed to go from Step Two to a Happy Ending.

I walked over to the phone and called the hotel. Nearly ten minutes later I finally reached the right person.

"No sir," I replied for the third time, "three rooms in the large hotel, four in the small one...and one in the large hotel should have space for a babysitter to sleep, as well as the children. No, sir,

I won't be sleeping next to the babysitter, my son will… No, sir, my son is not over 18. Yes, sir, the babysitter does know about this arrangement and approves. May I please speak with your colleague, Melanie, as I've already agreed on everything with her?"

To be fair, nothing was actually agreed on with her. I knew Melanie only by email. But I liked her name and her deep, charming voice, which I heard over a single phone call, and this gave me confidence. I decided to try the salesperson. A few minutes after this call, I got an email from Melanie finally confirming exactly what I wanted.

See, my darling? I'm a trustworthy gentleman! I told you two months ago that everything is under control. Aside from a few details, of course, like the final number of rooms and the lineup of who sleeps where and with whom. Not a problem, I know the guest list and the room reservations by heart, I would send Melanie an email with detailed instructions. Done and dusted.

Melanie's response swept me off my feet. "Are you sure this is final?"

Hello? Of course I'm sure. Absolutely.

Better double-check.

I called my ex-wife to be sure that she could drop off my children on the front steps of the hotel on the day before the wedding. Turns out they could only arrive on the day of the wedding. That meant that the children's room would be half-empty the night before. We were not about to pay for a half-empty room! I sent a text message to my sister, asking if she'd like to come a day early, as there would be a room free.

"Great," she wrote back.

I penned a new email to the hotel. "Dear Melanie, there is just one change, otherwise everything is 100% as I wrote it in the previous email."

Her reply did not sweep me off my feet this time. "Is this final now?"

My beauty stood beside me, breathing furiously through her nostrils and wondering what I was up to. What am I up to? I'm on top of everything, but she doesn't believe me.

"Call your best man and ask if he has a room," she hissed. Then the best possible future wife stomped out of the room.

Okay, okay. I called Mark, my best man. He would fulfill this role for me for the second time. After a few minutes, we learned that my betrothed was right. Again. Mark didn't have a room yet because he'd been shopping around for the best deal. We agreed to add him to my list because I was in communication with the hotel.

And so, a new email to Melanie.

Subject: "Kesar Wedding, final final!"

"Dear Melanie, we really did find one more change. Who would've thought, teeheehee :) In the attachment I'm sending you the final, final list with the number of rooms and their occupants. This is now 100%, as I've assured you several times over the phone. Thank you for your determination and I ask for the final confirmation from your end.

Yours Respectfully,

Kamenko Kesar"

A few minutes later, she replied.

"Okay, thank you. I will send you a pro forma invoice tomorrow. Before that I will ask you again for a final list. I'll wait until you're really sure."

At least I was sure of something about this project. Melanie was a tough nut to crack.

It'll Be Different When We're Married

Two weeks til showtime and it's flying by. Eight months back, on the first day of the new year, I suggested to the love of my life that we wed the same year, which would mean this past summer. Just as now it felt like it was ages ago that I'd made that suggestion, at that time it had felt an eternity to wait to get married. Now that eternity was only fourteen days away.

I'm neither a panicker nor a cryer. I'm a wonderer. And I was wondering. A lot. What good will this wedding bring me? What will I, a wild and crazy guy, weighing in at 98 kilos (215 pounds) and a towering 191 centimeters (6'2") tall, hairy and tattooed…what will I get from this wedding?

Let's say that if, as a married man, I have a nightmare and fall out of the bed. Will my beloved gently lift me back into our warm love nest, pull the blanket up to my chin, kiss the bump on my forehead and wish me sweet dreams?

Or if, as a married man, I wake hungry in the middle of the night, will my little bird feed me hearty, healthy food, perhaps chocolate (I like the ones with whole hazelnuts inside), while I cry on an empty stomach, pointing to my open mouth to indicate which of my basic needs is going unmet?

What if I, a married man, suddenly and for no good reason, God forbid, sneeze and have to go to the hospital. Will my kitten dress up as a nurse, prepare me medicine, sit beside me in bed and caress my brow? Will she proceed to slip off the blanket and unbutton her blouse and so on?

What if I, a married manly man, harpoon my own thumb while sewing a button on a shirt with a needle? Will my beauty remove her white blouse, tear it into strips and make a bandage of it, take my hand, place my wounded thumb in her mouth and lick the blood while looking up at me with those doe eyes? Will she caress my hair as I lie, pale, upon the bed? Will she smile as she realizes that, despite my suffering, I cannot take my eyes off her breasts? Will she assist by removing her bra, and so on?

What if I, married man that I shall be, decide to take the rubbish from our third floor shared apartment in the city center--at my own initiative, let it be said--then walk a full one-hundred meters (300 feet) to the dumpster, then back, then up three flights of stairs again; if I do all this, will she thank me and my self-sacrifice, and this in the middle of the week, in the afternoon, after a hard day at work?

What if I, as a married man, sit upon the couch beside our children and watch a cartoon with them: do I also get a bowl of cream of wheat? Will I be permitted to eat it on the couch, and not at the table, along with our little love bugs? Will she dab the corners of my mouth when I finish as she does theirs?

And what if I, being a married man, shout with too much enthusiasm while watching football? Will my darling dress in a miniskirt and tight t-shirt and bring me a cold beer and a cup of peanuts to soothe my aching vocal chords? Will she let me naughtily slap her ass? Will she, after I do so, smile at me and remove said tight t-shirt and so on?

What if I, a married man, find that I will, once married, have to act like a grownup?

The Wife is Always Right

Seven days til liftoff. Then I will become a husband. Alenka's husband. Husband of the soon-to-be Alenka Kesar. AK, who is 46 years young. That will make me the husband of an AK-46. Close enough.

I once had a partner with a similar name: she was an AK-47, aka Kalashnikov assault rifle. That was when I served my mandatory stint in the Yugoslav Army, back in 1988, when I was just eighteen years young. I took care of her. I undressed her in the evening, wiped her down, massaged her with oils, dressed her, stroked her and put her down for the night. From morning til evening we were an inseparable couple.

I carried her with me always and everywhere. But she was sometimes disobedient. And that was not my fault. I told her that the goal of target practice was to shoot the middle of the bullseye, but she chose to hit the haystack beside it. At the same time, she bruised my shoulder, a punch that told me to man up, hold me firmly yet gently at the same time! And be smart about it.

I didn't do well with her, I'll admit. Instead of gripping her with feeling, I squeezed her with all my might. I sought to tame her. Like a real man, a muscly man. But she bruised me even more. After a year or so, we went our separate ways. Neither of us were willing to yield and meet the other halfway. And my right shoulder was still bruised.

Twenty-eight years later, I will be marrying her cousin, AK-46, a partner who taught me how to squeeze her tightly yet hold her gently at the same time. A partner who always hits the bullseye. I take care of her. In the evening I undress her, I wipe her down, I massage her with oils and in the morning she dresses again.

I still have a lot of work to do in one very special department. After the wedding, I will no longer be able to refer to her as my girlfriend or mistress. I'm going to have to call her my wife. This will be a significant shift in vocabulary for me.

"Wife," I shall say unto her, "where is the remote?" This was the most frequently-uttered phrase by my father. I've never asked my beauty this question. Instead, I look for it myself. I usually start looking underneath my beauty, in case she is seated upon it, and continue the search up her shirt, in case that naughty remote has taken to hiding therein. Truth be told, I've never once found it there, but it's the journey, not the destination, as wise men say.

"Wife," I shall say unto her, "fetch me a beer, posthaste." This would also be a novelty in our family. Maybe it's because I've never been a beer drinker, but around these parts, it's a commonly-used phrase among married men, or so I'm told. I, as a newly-married man, must learn from my predecessors.

And will her inviting "Honeybun, come to the table, breakfast is served" be replaced by a grumpy wife, post-wedding, muttering "What's for breakfast?"

We've been so sweet as boyfriend and girlfriend. Now, if the internet is to be believed (and I'm told it's never wrong), and the elderly confirm this, I will be the one who should mutter "What's for breakfast?" And I should ask about everything. "Wife, why won't the car start? Wife, why is the car in first gear? Wife, why isn't the car in first gear?" This, it would seem, is the key ingredient to a happy marriage. Constant inquiry.

I'm told that pet names will also change. Gone will be the days of "beauty, sweetheart, kitten, babe." From the wedding Saturday forth, we will refer to one another exclusively as "wife, wifey and, of course, Her Royal Wifeness." The point being that it must always be clear that she is my wife. I will finally be able to stop lying to children and parents alike that we are not having sex. I'm told by married colleagues that married couples, it is safe to assume, do have sex, even if they do not. Yes, everything will be different after the wedding.

"I'll call my husband," is a popular post-wedding threat wielded by new wives. "My husband will fix it" is a sentence that injects said husband with pride, this perhaps unmerited confidence that I'll be able to sort out anything and everything.

Last but not least, there are two phrases that will put things in their proper place. They are the alpha and omega of married life. They are shields and swords, to cut through any Gordian knot that life may throw at us, and to deflect the slings and arrows. These two phrases are:

"I'll ask my wife."

"Wife, you are right."

My future depends on these two phrases.

After the wedding, which is to say in seven days, I will always ask my wife what to do, when to do it and whether or not to do it at all. I will trust her to decide for our collective good. My wife will always be right after the wedding.

But until then...

The Wedding

We finished the last bottle of wine. It was 6:15 and the first tourists drifted past the hotel terrace towards the bakery, while others set off on a morning run. My wife and I hugged.

"Husband, should we go upstairs?"

I nodded. The last sweet act of a wondrous and memorable wedding awaited us. We'd been up all night and bid farewell to the friends who had weathered the duration of the party with us. Up to our hotel room.

We jumped into the shower and then into bed.

Three hours later, my ankle-length eyelids and I stood downstairs in the hotel's breakfast room. Friends smiled at us. Someone patted me on the shoulder. "Dude, rough night, huh?" he said."I hope it was wild." Then he zipped off to the coffee machine.

I smiled to myself. It really was wild.

We did a lot of things that night.

Everything except that.

Who has the energy?

Honeymoon

It remains a mystery to me how we ended up honeymooning on the small island of Lopud, near Dubrovnik on the Croatian coast. I remember we started out with a plan for the Maldives, then shifted to Bali. Madagascar was a strong candidate for a while. Three months later? Lopud.

It's a beautiful island, don't get me wrong. A cove, a clutch of houses, a few cafes and a supermarket. No cars because there are no roads. A lot of wheelbarrows and bicycles and the occasional golf cart, shuttling between the village and the beach.

The British Telegraph newspaper ranked this beach among the most beautiful on the Adriatic. We hadn't heard of this island before that, and certainly not this particular beach. But with such strong marketing we figured it was time to try her out. On the second day of the honeymoon, just after a refreshing sleep, we went from the Lafodia Hotel to the Dubrovnik Restaurant, from whence we turned right and walked about ten meters (30 feet) to a funny, battery-powered car. The driver was just on his way home, but did us a favor and let us hitch a ride to heaven on earth. Within those few minutes together, he explained that his grandfather owned a village near Dubrovnik, along with who knows what else, and that his mother and sister lived on this island...and that he'd quarrelled with everyone and they'd forgotten him, pretending he didn't exist, but that it was fine with him. So he drives an e-taxi and rents rooms and a speedboat with, he said, the fastest motor on the Adriatic.

A moment later we arrived at the beach. An ordinary beach with mangled deckchairs. All the anticipated magic disappeared. Had we expected too much? Dripping with disappointment, we morosely waded into the water and, before we got even up to our knees, turned around, hired the e-taxi and headed back to the hotel. We'd spent less than five minutes on the Telegraph's most beautiful beach on the Adriatic.

Disappointed with what we saw, we decided to drown our sorrows with a snack at our hotel's beach. Branimir, our friendly waiter, approached. We chatted. My darling ate a club sandwich, I a greasy burger. We asked Branimir to send our bill to the room.

"Sure, to the room," he replied. "Whose room? Yours? Mine?"

I thought it was a decent joke and laughed. My wife looked at me as if a sea cucumber was growing out of my nose.

"It's all the same to me," I said, "my room is 352. And yours?"

"135," said Branimir.

We smiled. I told him that he surely doesn't live at the hotel, if he's a waiter. He laughed again and said he did have a room there, but we agreed that, this time at least, the bill should be sent to my room. I signed the bill and we said goodbye.

My blushing bride was still staring at me, a what-the-fuck-is-wrong-with-you look. "Now you're going to flirt with waiters," she said? "And you're newly-married, you bonehead."

I wasn't bothered at the time by my bride's jibes. I checked off another box on my bucket list. For the first time on vacation, I'd managed to get a stranger's room number.

Swapping an Englishwoman

Three days after the wedding we were lying on the hotel's beach. Very much married.

Ringed hand on my heart, I must say that I'd not yet gotten used to married life. So my wife did me the favor of reminding me, at every opportunity, that it was no longer going to be the way it had been. For example, she just walked over to me and hissed, "What's the deal, Kesar, you're not going to give me a like?"

I quickly opened Facebook on my phone and "liked" the photo she'd posted thirty seconds ago.

"Now that we're married I'm going to have to ask you to like my photos? That's how this is gonna roll now, is it?"

I tried to explain to her that thirty seconds is too little a reaction time to allot me. She should give me at least an hour before bringing down the hammer.

"You no longer have an hour, Kesar, you're my husband now."

That morning we spotted a lot of empty deckchairs on the beach, which the guests had "reserved" by laying hotel towels upon them. On the Croatian coast, this is a tourist ritual. The woman rises at six in the morning and folds the towels into a large backpack. They hop down to the beach and choose the very empty deckchairs that they like best. One for each family member. They place towels on them, line them up nicely and head back to the hotel room. Around nine, three hours later, the whole family adjourns to the breakfast room and, by ten, to the still-almost-empty beach. There are the deckchairs waiting for them and some of us honest idiots are seated on pebbles by the sea because all the deckchairs were "occupied."

"Kesar, you know what you have to do tomorrow," said my wife, pointing to the occupied deckchairs.

"Not that, my dear," I replied. "I refuse to get up early and reserve with towels. It's not fair and it's not me."

"I have to do everything myself!" my love erupted in reply, then set an early alarm on her phone for the next day.

The next morning, after breakfast, we were lucky enough to find two free deckchairs and a parasol in the front row on the beach. We lay our towels down when a lady about our age, with an English accent, approached. Well, maybe she was younger than we were, because the English tend to look older than we Balkaners.

"Might we switch positions with her?" She was thoroughly irritated. I politely asked her to explain what the problem was.

"You see, my parasol lounger is here next to a friend's lounger. Theirs is okay and my parasol casts a shadow on a wooden platform three feet away in the morning, and I can't move my lounger there because people walk there. If we could switch it'd be brilliant because your loungers are next to my friend and because I imagine you won't want to lie in the shade, whereas I would."

Of course, madam, we're tomatoes and we like the sun.

We didn't switch.

We straightened the towels on our deckchairs, took out of our bag what was to be taken out of our bag, held hands and slowly walked out to the sea. Purely driven by curiosity, we stopped a few feet in and looked back to check on what our new acquaintance was doing, since we'd denied her request.

It was quite a site. The woman, like some chessmaster, had negotiated with and shifted around innumerable other guests on their deckchairs in order to snake her way over to the shade beside her friend. She got one guest after another to accept a deckchair switch with her, each time getting closer to her friend. But she would encounter other "stubborn" guests, like us, who would not accept her proposal and so she'd have to figure out a different route.

Meanwhile, my wife and I bathed and emerged from the water. We solved a crossword puzzle, read a few chapters in a book, went back in for a dip. The lady was still flying up and down the beach. I watched her pause, draw up a new plan of attack as she calculated the minimum number of position swaps needed to reach her goal, and lurked until the owners of the impeding towels in question returned to them. About half of the beach's populace accepted. It took her about an hour, but she finally succeeded. She stood proudly by her deckchair in the shade, beside her friend. With her head raised and her hands on her hips, she monitored her domain, nodded contentedly...then left the beach.

Everything's a Competition

One week after the wedding, and I can report that everything has shifted precisely as predicted by my friends, relatives, my wife, even passing acquaintances. In short, everyone except me.

The direction was clear. My wife was now fully in charge. She knew best when I should sleep, what and when I should eat, when I woke too early in the morning, that iced coffee was the best option for me to order (two a day, to be precise) and how often I should go for a swim. I also had the feeling that she was speaking ever more quietly with me. This was probably to encourage me to look at her directly, so she'd have my full attention if there was something she wanted. For example, yesterday she whispered something about being thirsty then wondered why I did not suddenly materialize by her side, beverage in hand.

But the man within me did not give up. I told her clearly today... well, maybe I didn't so much tell her, but I showed her that I would go swimming when, and as often, as I liked. I rose from the deck-chair, determined and moving with confidence, and set out for the sea. I did not hesitate, in order not to show any weakness. I stepped to the edge of the water and dipped my big toe in. Just to show that I can. That was all. With a rooster's strut, I turned around and retreated to our checkchairs. My beauty didn't even move. Dammit, she'd been so immersed in her book she hadn't even noticed. I slowly returned to her side, stepped majestically before her and, before I could say anything, without looking away from the book, she coldly and quietly stated, "I'm thirsty. Go get some water, since you're standing. But be careful not to slop. It's dangerous to walk on tiles with a wet right big toe."

I managed to make it to the outdoor bar, leaned against it, and waited my turn.

"Iced coffee please, with vanilla ice cream, no ice."

The waiter paused for a moment, looked at me as if he had never seen a Slovene on his beach before, and replied, "Alas and alack, what will they think of next? He wants iced coffee without ice."

I returned to my wife just as a daily group engaged in water aerobics, led by a sympathetic, smiling young man. They bent and stretched in the surf in front of our deckchairs. My darling noticed this young man immediately.

"Look, Kesar!" She elbowed me under the ribs. I looked up and saw the aerobics coach playing with a small child who kept bringing him pebbles from the beach, stacking them diligently beside the coach's notebook. The young man was patient, even smiling. The whole time. My darling glowed.

"Look, Kesar, and learn from the best. Be kind to small children and any woman will swoon before you."

I looked at her from beneath a furrowed brow. Oh really, my look retorted, if I'm kind to small children you'll swoon? For me?

"Yes," replied my bride, reading my thoughts, "just not for you. You're married now."

"Dear gentlemen, but especially dear ladies," the coach began to announce. My darling giggled and toyed with her hair.

"I'm going to get some exercise, Kesar," she said. "Good that I thought to put on makeup today."

I looked at her as if she'd fallen from outer space. My wife? Exercise?

"Kesar, how's my hair?" She did not wait for my response. She straightened her hat, walked past the small child, stroking his hair, swung her gaze toward the coach, smiled at him, and dove into the water like a young doe. The first of anyone to join in.

That evening we went out for pizza. My wife took my hand, slowed her pace, and said, "My muscles are aching. From water aerobics."

"I bet. Why did you exercise so, uh, vigorously?"

"Kesar, you understand nothing. There were only young doves

around me. I had to show that I could handle them."

I looked at her in amazement.

"It's all a competition, Kesar. Everything."

Electricity

One morning we were greeted with a lack of electricity. Everything suddenly switched off. Obviously, because our entire life runs on electricity.

When the electricity went out, the wife and I were getting ready for breakfast. I was dressed and standing in the middle of the hotel room, while my beauty anointed herself with ablutions in the bathroom. This is the state of affairs most likely to swiftly enrage my beloved. I, standing there, imply that she should hurry up. Then the electricity went out.

My angel turned on me in an instant and shouted to turn the goddamn light back on because I was driving her nuts again. I could barely convince her that it wasn't me playing with the light switch. As soon as we reconciled, she was ready with a new demand.

"The air conditioning won't work either? You'll make sure that our room stays nice and cool, won't you?"

Yes darling. Of course I will.

Down in the breakfast room, the guests were standing around something, slightly bent over, everyone looking in the same direction, towards the buffet. The guest at the head of the buffet line slowly straightened up, turned toward the crowd, nodded and made his move. He walked over to the fruit selection, picked up an apple, and sat down at a table. The guests at the aforementioned buffet were dissatisfied with this. Another guest charged forward and began to do something or other at the buffet. The other waited in rapt silence. And waited. The guest straightened up after a few moments, also nodded, and made his way to a table. The crowd murmured in desperation and slowly moved away from the buffet. There, at the spot around which the crowd had gathered, the technological wonder sat lonely and abandoned. A miracle without electricity is but a hope-smashing disappointment for mankind.

A non-functioning waffle iron.

Beauty, the Old Man and the Sea

On the final afternoon of our honeymoon, my bride was not feeling well. She sent me to the beach on my own. These represented the first hours of marriage that we did not spend together. It seemed so very adventurous to wander the world alone but married, but I did not reveal my curiosity and enthusiasm to experiment with this sensation. With a towel and literature in hand, I calmly kissed her goodbye and sought the sea.

Somewhere towards the end of the beach, I found a pile of empty deckchairs and shade. There was no one around. I set one of the deckchairs to aim towards the sea, put my belongings onto it and headed into the water. A few minutes later I lay upon my deckchair, wet and pleasantly tired. I picked up the book and started reading. After a few chapters, my phone rang.

The wife.

"Where are you, sweetheart?"

"On the beach, in the shade, on a deckchair, my love."

"What are you doing?"

"Well, I'm pretending to read a book," I joked, "but I'm actually checking out the babes."

"A lot of good it'll do you, poor man."

How quickly my joke soured into truth. I put the phone down on the towel and noticed that one babe, around thirty years old, max, was walking towards me. Wide hips, great tits, sunglasses and, over the swimsuit, a see-through teddy sort of a dress. She stopped at the deckchair behind mine and put down her bag. She removed her teddy sort of a dress and walked slowly towards the sea. Narrow of waist, womanly of posterior. A real feminine rhythm. The babe stepped into the water and, without stopping, ploughed headlong into the waves. I looked away from her and sank back into my book.

A minute later a gentleman, maybe sixty years old, walked past me wearing brown Bermuda shorts. He was hairless, his own set of tits sagging, stick insect legs swaying from under a considerable belly. The gentleman jumped into the water and swam towards her.

They met at a red buoy and started kissing. The babe giggled audibly and he joked. English. She was growing ever more exuberant, diving down, swimming away, then circling back for a kiss. They bobbed in the water, cuddling and kissing. Then kissing some more.

At one point, they calmed down. She clung tightly to him. She rested her head on his cheek. The wind blowing inland carried with it the sound of a moan. She squeezed even closer to him, her eyes closed, her mouth slightly open. I couldn't imagine they were actually in flagrante delicto, because I couldn't imagine the man could reach the sea floor with his feet and he surely couldn't tread water that long and keep thrusting. I noticed that both of them were staying afloat by paddling with one arm.

Suddenly they moved away from each other and slowly swam towards shore. That was when my darling joined me on the deckchair. I quickly explained the situation to her. The gentleman and the babe swam in close enough that the gentleman could stand. They were some ten meters (30 feet) away from us. She clung to him, pressed her head to his cheek again and closed her eyes.

My wife and I looked at each other. Classic aquatic intercourse.

After a few minutes, the gentleman stepped out of the water. He covered the front of his swimsuit with both hands. He walked over to the deckchair and grabbed a towel. I estimated that he was hiding an appendage that was at least 20 centimeters (half a foot) long and as thick as a forearm. His brown Bermuda shorts could barely keep the beast in place.

My love and I had wondered how such a beauty could end up with this old man. There was our answer, in all its flagpole glory. We got up and walked back to the hotel in awed silence.

Tip of the Day: Never Into the Wind!

On Thursday, the day before leaving Lopud, my beauty and I sat on the beach. It was about ten in the morning when I suddenly thought we had to go home. A day before we actually had to. The thought emerged of its own volition. We figured that we had to gather our things quickly, pack up and there were only two hours until the only ferry of the day departed. But we decided to stay. For an "extra" day.

My alarm clock rang the next morning at ten past five. I tended to my morning routine, minus breakfast. You can't get food at the hotel at this hour, aside from a pre-ordered bagged meal.

At ten to six, we walked the kilometer (half a mile) to the ferry. The hotel did not want to help us with our luggage because we'd opted for public transport, which would cost us 3 Euros each. If we'd gone in their boat, they would've been happy to help with the luggage because it would have cost us 45 Euros each. They told us they weren't allowed to drive us any other way, as there was a ban on cars. The whole street was full of cars, but apparently the hotel wasn't allowed.

At twenty past six, we downed our first proper espresso in two weeks, at the ferry bar. Less than an hour later, we landed in Dubrovnik, paid for our long-term parking, spent five minutes cleaning pine needle gunk off the windshield, and we were on our way.

Ten minutes later, I enthusiastically pointed out a set of houses where I'd stayed during my high school graduation student trip and I'd met a Slovenian babe. When I'd cologned myself for the evening party, I'd missed my armpit and maced myself in the eyes. I walked around that night with sunglasses on.

We stopped at the first gas station, bought two large coffees, plus two backup coffees, some pre-made ham and cheese sandwiches and a water bottle. On our way out, we got the idea that we could make our own jam if we got some local apricots. We'd spotted some fruit stalls along the road on our way in, and we hoped they would still be there. They were.

We stopped at the first one and bought a whole crate of apricots, 20 kilos' (44 pounds) worth. The vendor was so surprised that he didn't even say goodbye, but immediately flew to his phone to tell his wife the news. Then we went to the next stall to make another purchase. At this point, I will pass the mic to my wife, because she interpreted the following event rather differently than I.

We stopped at another fruit stall by the road. Behind the stall stood a young, lovely girl with long lashes and a dress that hung off her shoulders. Very cute. She took one look at Kamenko, adjusted her dress to hang lower off her shoulders and smiled broadly.

"What would you like?" she inquired demurely.

"Apricots," I replied.

"May I try one?" Kamenko asked her.

"Well of course you can," she replied, smiling at him.

We tried her apricots. They were severely sour. The girl saw our expressions and said, "Is it sour? Well, it's not ripe yet. I mean, it hasn't been in the sun long enough. I mean, they were picked..."

She blushed and looked at Kamenko. "I'm sorry," she said, "I'm a little dazed."

Kamenko laughed his most charming laugh. I thought I would barf. The girl looked at him with those big, beautiful eyes and continued, "Well, I don't know what's wrong with me today."

I know what's wrong with you, I thought. I couldn't believe how charmingly she fluttered her eyelashes at him, right in front of me, his wife. Out of courtesy we bought some nectarines. Back at the car, I said to my husband, "She was pretty cute, huh?"

The idiot looked at me. "Yes...well...yes...yes..."

"See how much she liked you?" I continued.

The idiot: "What? No! You're imagining..."

How nice it is to have a blind husband.

So we bought three crates in the end. There was a cute girl at the last stall. She knew a priest from back home who Alenka knew. She and Alenka had a connection, so Alenka bought an extra liter of schnapps. We spent so much that she even gave us a free bag of peaches and plums, on the house.

Around eleven we drove towards the town of Zadar and spotted a fire off to the right side of the highway. The wind blew brown smoke across the road, which meant that the traffic would come to a halt very soon. And so it was. Behind us, a section of the highway was closed due to fire. Ahead of us, it was closed due to gale force winds and a pair of accidents. It was four hours after we'd left Dubrovnik, at fifteen to twelve, just ten kilometers (6 miles) before the exit for Zadar, and everything stood still.

Around half past eight, we stopped in a village. Along the road, 200 meters ahead of us, was a store that was closed. A half hour later we were about 50 meters from the aforementioned store. The owner came and opened it. Neighbors had summoned the owner because those of us stuck in our cars were hungry. We rushed inside and grabbed something edible. I bought two packets of prosciutto and cheese, crackers, Coke and chocolate. All the while, the traffic was motionless.

Truth be told, the biggest issue was peeing. We men could step to the highway barrier, turn our backs to the road, and let'er rip. The ladies, however, couldn't manage any such trick without providing a free show.

At one point, my dearest took my hand and said, "I have to pee."

We looked around. There were people everywhere, many standing outside of their cars because their cars were in no danger of having to move anytime soon.

"I'm gonna do it in the back seat," she said, placing a coffee cup in my hands. I noticed there was still some coffee in it, so I drank it, figuring it was better now than later. My dove dropped her trousers and shorts in the back seat, set up the coffee cup and let'er rip.

"Another, Kesar, another!" she suddenly cried out and passed me the first, which was full to the brim.

We swapped cups. If anyone happened to look into the car at that moment, they would've thought I was raising the cup in a celebratory toast. The wife filled cup number two. Luckily, a third wasn't needed.

She dressed, stepped outside, and disposed of the cup contents by the side of the road. I watched my lovely bride, noticing that both of her trouser legs were soaked.

"Screw it," she said with a wave of her hand, "next time I'll aim better."

Next time occurred two hours later. We followed the same routine, including the cup swap. It was a faster procedure, but no more on target. She was likewise soaked.

"You whizzed on yourself again," I said. "How is that possible if you had your trousers around your ankles?"

"But I didn't hit my thighs. I would've felt that."

After inching forward some 60 meters (200 feet), I turned to the back seat, where my darling had relieved herself. There, as if it had miraculously materialized, lay a large, ripe peach.

I had no troubles to report, in the peeing department. Everything went like clockwork. I correctly calculated trajectory and wind speed and viewing angle so I would not show the occupants of other cars my wang. This functioned several times during this long, slow drive home, aside from once, the final time. Unfortunately I shot in completely the wrong direction. As usual, I did my wind calculations first. Then I unzipped and let forth my stream. Somewhere halfway through, when I was already too relaxed, a crazy gust of wind pushed me forward, while a second gust in the other direction tipped me back. Then a third gust seemed to rise from beneath me. My stream streamed upwards, showering my chest and even my face. It happened so quickly that I was still flowing for a few more seconds before I realized that the refreshing shower I felt upon my sweaty brow was not a sudden, welcome rainfall.

Soaked, I returned to the car, sat heavily and with a squish, and requested all the tissues we had. I wipe my glasses. My darling was just about to comment, when I preempted her. "Do not ask. Ever."

PART THREE

Life Together

Ever Since I've Been Married

Nine weeks post-wedding and things are finally falling into place. Some turned out for the better, others for the worse. On the good side of the equation, the bed was always warm. On the not-so-good side, I screwed up by purchasing a bed that was too wide. Some nights we slept so far apart that I wasn't sure if my wife was even sleeping in the same room. I stopped begging for sex. Of course I did, now we were married. Now at night I would squeeze myself onto the far edge of the oversized bed and lay there, motionless, hoping for her to remember I was there. If she didn't, I flipped and spun around until she got annoyed and hissed, "What is it? You wanna have sex or something?"

"Yes, my dear, my beauty, thank you for asking."

I also started to count my underwear. I don't know how, but the best ones, by which I mean the comfiest and softest, mysteriously disappeared after the wedding, each time they went to the laundry. My wife assured me that this was no unsolved mystery. At the same time, she mentioned how heartwarming she found our life together. Apparently, it was also kidney-warming.

I never admitted I was hungry. Or perhaps I didn't phrase that correctly? Whenever I mentioned I was hungry, my wife placed a shopping list into my warm palm and sent me to the store. I stopped complaining. But if she volunteered and asked me if I was hungry, I vigorously nodded in the affirmative.

Ever since our marriage, I've been witness to supernatural activities. My wife's hearing enhanced to 110% normal human capacity. She hears all that I say plus even what I think but do not articulate.

Her car has also become my car. Even before, it was hardly flawless, from a cosmetic standpoint. It was lightly buffed at the corners. Love scratches at the doors. And the bumpers. And the chassis. All this was our new reality. We Kesars had a sterling reputation in the driving department, now ruined by our wedlock.

In this spirit, contemplating the positives and the negatives, I've found that my wife is less sensitive than I first thought. For example, yesterday she called me to come to a parking lot in the city center to solve a situation.

"This guy who parked along the road claims that I scratched his car!"

A few minutes later, there I was, standing at the scene of the alleged accident. The guy explained to me, at length, that he was sitting innocently in his car when something rubbed against it. My wife listened calmly for a while, then shrugged anemically. "I didn't feel a thing."

A few days prior, at the mall, her left front wheel got caught in a chain and dragged it along behind her. The chain was attached, on its other end, to a lump of concrete, which was thumping along as she drove. A friend who was riding shotgun while my bride drove asked her to stop the car to see what all that clunking was. My wife got out of the car, spotted the chain wrapped around the wheel, and the lump of concrete at the end of the chain, and commented, "I guess that's it. Well, I didn't feel a thing."

Ever since I heard that, during each evening's bedroom melee, I'll stop frequently to ask if my wife is feeling anything. I refuse to continue until she confirms.

Two Forks

My darling and I decided to take advantage of a generous wedding gift from our friends, Spela and Robi: a visit to a spa in the beautiful town of Bled, including a sauna, massage and swim in the pool. We're not regular visitors to saunas, as we don't handle the heat well. We're not regular visitors to massages, as we don't handle the pain well. We're not regular visitors to swimming pools, as we don't handle the hostile looks of fellow swimmers well when we pee in it. Otherwise, this was a perfect gift.

Nevertheless, my love and I were undeterred and made a reservation. After a delicious lunch, we set off on our pampering expedition.

We arrived on Lake Bled a half an hour early. The wife suggested we go to the famous Park Hotel to indulge in their famous dessert, Bled Cream Cake. She said that she was sure to sweat off any calories she added now, so eating pre-sauna seemed like a fine strategy. This sounded entirely logical to me, so I agreed. We sat on the hotel terrace overlooking the lake and summoned the waitress.

"I'll take an espresso filled to the top of the cup," I said.

"Me, too," said my wife, "plus a Cream Cake."

"Will you take a Cream Cake, too?" the waitress asked me.

"No thank you," I said, "I'm not hungry." My assassin eyes warned her not to probe further. She did not heed my warning.

"You need to be hungry to enjoy a Cream Cake?" she dared continue.

"No, just not in the mood," I confirmed.

"Shall I bring two forks?" the waitress boldly ventured.

My wife jerked her head towards the waitress, Exorcist style, and hissed through clenched teeth, "Not on your life! If he doesn't want it, he doesn't get it!"

This seemed an overly-emotional response to me.

"You have to be hungry for Cream Cake," she mumbled to herself. I wasn't clear how I'd screwed up, but the screwing in an upward direction was clear.

The waitress brought the Cream Cake...with two forks. My wife grabbed both with cobra-like reflexes I didn't know she had. She dove into the cake with a fork in each hand, scooping first with one fork, then the other. I watched her with my tail between my legs, awaiting the inevitable offer: "Want some?" But it was all quiet on the western front.

The final bites approaching, she looked up from the plate at me and winked.

"What? You want a bite?"

I smiled. At last, proof of her undying love. She asked me.

"Well, I would, actually..."

"Well, you won't," she said, snarfing the rest of the cake into her mouth until the plate shone.

We set off for our spa experience, one of us hungry, the other angry. Never a good combination.

A Man With a Cold is No Man At All

I lay in bed, feverish and coughing, on my birthday. I thought about my life and why I decided to write stories about it. I also pondered the question of why the most important opinion of all was that of my bride, who took care of me all weekend long, she who knew exactly how I was feeling.

I wasn't really exactly feverish, nor did I cough excessively. But I did feel like a real man does when he's attacked by a virus or bacteria...really anything so much smaller than we are that we can't possibly knock them out or kick them aside. I recalled the words of my loving wife on our wedding day: "I will care for you for the rest of my life."

Given that I am so rarely ill, I figured I should take every opportunity for her to treat me like a lap dog.

So we were lying on the couch in our warm country house. I had a cold, which meant that I was thoroughly unoperational as a man. My love stepped up her game and organized pills, powders and healing beverages for me.

"Take these every two hours, this one once a day, these two in combination, under the tongue and no biting. This is the proper medicine, and these little balls..." They looked like albino hamster droppings. "...they're a homeopathic alternative, you slip this one under your tongue, this one goes in your anus..."

Hang on. Back that up a minute.

"Sorry," she corrected, "you're not under three years old anymore, at least not most of the time, so I'll crush it and you'll sniff it."

For a moment it seemed to me that I'd lost consciousness due to some terrible disease. A flash of light burst before my eyes, with utter darkness beyond.

"Oh my god," I thought in horror, "not now, not while I'm lying down. If I lie down, my wife will not notice that anything's happened to me." I had to get up because I wanted to fall to the ground if I were to faint, possibly knocking myself (slightly) on the way down, so I would provoke even more of her welcome sympathy. I grabbed the edge of the couch and slowly straightened up. I saw light bursts in darkness, a devilish darkness, the foreplay of bestial suffering and hellish toments, the foretaste of smashed skulls and cracked bones. I took a deep breath and tried to faint, but my darling grabbed my arm, pulled me into the hallway, and ordered, drill-sergeant-style, "We lost electricity which means the heating's dead. Pack up, we're going back to the city."

This confused me. I wasn't quite sure I understood what she meant, as I was still on the edge of consciousness. I coughed lightly. She didn't hear me. She couldn't tell if I'd coughed or if a snow-heavy branch had broken off a nearby spruce tree. I staggered towards the fuse box, emphasizing my stagger so she wouldn't think I was suddenly healthy or anything like that.

We climbed into the car. Snow lay thick around us. As soon as she looked at me in the driver's seat, I saw fear in her eyes. "I'll take care of you, don't worry. Just drive slowly and leave the rest to me."

I was reassured.

We inched down the road. I hadn't put chains on the tires because I'd been on sick leave and I hadn't the strength. Even before the first bend, we came across two trees that had fallen across the road. We couldn't possibly go any further. My doe sighed.

"My poor thing," she said, stroking my face.

"I know, darling," I replied with elegant stoicism, "we're stuck, I'm sick and you're beautiful."

I reached for my phone to inform the fire department when the wife slowly leaned over and whispered in my ear. "Put your hood up so you don't get your hair wet."

It took me a moment to register what she was thinking. Could she be implying that I, in my unwell state, should exit the car and try to shift the fallen trees myself?

"If you want, I'll help you," she helpfully added while looking at her feet, shedding the tears of a helpless woman whose very life is in the hands of a Real Man. She squeezed my palm. Her eyes roamed the depths of mine in search of hope. My wife wanted, nay needed, me to carry her to safety.

I took a deep breath, pulled my hood over my head. My wife was right. I am a man. A sick man, but a Man all the same. My embrace is warm and safe. My task is to overcome nature itself. I leapt out of the car, perhaps a little too quickly, to give the illusion of being totally healthy. I grabbed the first fallen tree and, with near super-human strength, I slowly moved it toward the edge of the road. As I did this, I watched her sit in the warm car, soothed by the rhythm of the wipers, as she manicured her nails. I understood her: what else was she to do in the wilderness, surrounded by arctic tempera-tures? My beauty noticed me noticing her.

"Need a hand?"

"No, my dove, you might injure yourself," I replied in my manliest baritone. Despite my muscle and ferocious toil, I could not shift the fatter fallen tree. I would have to drive off-road, over the neigh-bor's hedges, which meant that I desperately needed snow chains in place. I called to my bride, "I'll put the chains on!"

My bride nodded.

"Need a hand?"

"No, my dove, you might get sick!"

I climbed towards the trunk but slipped on an icy patch and end-ed up under the car. I wanted to play dead, but my darling hadn't noticed I'd fallen. I muscled the snow chains into place, wiped the frozen froth from my blue lips and smiled at her. Soaked and shiv-ering, I sat heavily in the car once more and we continued on our way. At least to the next bend. There we found yet another young spruce tree that had decided to faint across the road.

I felt her gaze upon me. Yes, yes, no need for words, my pet. I know: hood up and make like a lumberjack.

The Heart Speaks

"I feel like my heart thunders every now and then," my dearest confided in me anxiously at the beginning of the week. She grabbed the phone and called the one man who could help her.

Two days later, my doe returned from the doctor's office and jumped on me. I noticed that her neck, front and back, was covered with a bandage. Happy as an artificial resuscitator, she exclaimed, "Look!" and lifted her shirt.

"Holy shit!" I shouted, recoiling.

She looked like a terrorist, wired to blow. Wires and white patches stuck to her chest. Each patch was connected to a thin wire that ran into a thicker one. It reminded me of those programmable Legos. At the end of the wide wire, tucked into the elastic band of her undies, was a black plastic box.

"Look what I got," my bride sang in delight. I wasn't amused. All those wires made it look like a misplaced sneeze would end with us in bite-sized pieces. "I got a holter monitor so they can measure my heart activity 24 hours a day!" The Terminator continued, stretching her arms out in front of her and doing a squat. "I have to be fully active for the next 24 hours." She bowed. "The doctor said I have to strain my heart, so I'm going to be walking upstairs a lot."

"Wait a minute," I finally said, when I emerged from my hiding spot behind a door. "You have to be fully active for the next 24 hours?"

"Yes," she said, winking seductively a few times more than a non-cyborg should.

"In the evening, too. Not just during the day?" I was now fully visible, the door no longer shielding any part of my body.

"24 hours, doctor's orders."

A smile spread across my otherwise concerned visage.

"Why are you splitting like a sliced tomato?" she inquired.

"No reason, my pet."

Suddenly she realized. "Yes, Kesar, we also must include sexual activity within these 24 hours, if that's what you were thinking. Vigorous intercourse. As many activities as possible that cause the heart to beat like mad. So it's better for you to make an effort today and not embarrass me when the doctor examines the results."

I walked over and hugged her gently. In good times and bad, we promised each other. If my wife had to keep an elevated heart rate, I would be the first to volunteer to assist.

That whole day that my wife was wired I fantasized about the reaction tomorrow. I pictured her, tired and scruffy but thoroughly satisfied, arriving at the doctor's office with her holter monitor. A doctor and a gaggle of buxom nurses would gather around a large computer screen. The doctor would remove the memory card from the holter monitor and insert it into the computer. The data would upload. Before the graph of the 24-hour period displayed, a warning sign would appear on the screen: "In order for this graph to display properly, please mount an additional screen on top of it." The assembly whispers among themselves in awe. They bring in a second computer screen and set it up above the first.

The computer churns out the data, mapping it on the graph. The bottom screen shows the stair-walking, up and down. Some rest, some squats, more stairs, ten minutes of brisk walking... This is all leading up through the afternoon. Just before nightfall, the heart rate drops steeply for a good hour (my darling was cooking dinner and tidying up our apartment, which apparently she finds soothing). There's a short upward swing (showering, brushing her teeth).

Then the top screen switches on. The activity of her heart sinks but then sharply skyrockets to the top of the upper screen. It calms for a moment, then shoots higher still. And again. And again. The nurses tug at their collars and the doctor nods in approval.

I tore myself away from my thoughts. The wife and I were still standing in the middle of the room, hugging in silence. Yes, Kesar, it needs to be tested. But it was clear to me that evening action alone would be insufficient for proper testing. What happens before nightfall is equally critical to a sound analysis. If I wanted to achieve the right effect at the moment of truth, I had to ensure that my bride was calm beforehand. I had to ease her heart activity down to the lowest healthful point. My darling mustn't burden herself in any way. I shall be her only burden when the time is ripe.

My plan was organized and implemented to the last detail. Her final hour before bedtime passed in a mortuary peace. At the stroke of 10:57pm the in-bed action began. A proud 25 minutes later, it ended. My heart, at least, was hammering a mile a minute. When I finally regained some self-awareness, my darling and I embraced, winked at one another, switched off the light and fell asleep.

The next morning, my doe returned from the doctor's office and jumped on me. There were no more patches stuck to her neck. Happy as a bird in springtime, she lifted her shirt and said, "Behold!"

I beheld a pair of tits. Without patches.

My beautiful love hugged me. It was nice to see her so happy, but I really couldn't have cared less about her mood. I was only interested in what the doctor had said about the Mount Everest of a heart rate at, oh, say, 10:57pm-ish.

"What did they say?" I inquired casually.

The wife looked at me with shining eyes, kissed me gently and whispered into my ear, "They say that sex suits me. It has a highly beneficial effect."

I stared at her in surprise. "Hang on! Sex has a beneficial effect?"

"Yes, my love. We will continue to have sex," she mused. "Lots of sex. The monitor clearly demonstrated that it calmed my heart rate."

Porn is Always Plan B

When the Devil had offspring, he had them for two weeks straight. A hard-partying virus gleefully leapt from one member of our family to the next. Everyone was laid low. Only I was spared.

One afternoon, my beauty and I lay upon the couch.

"I'm going out with friends tonight," she said.

I tried to hide my smile. "Okay," I replied, inhaling slowly and deeply. I could hardly believe it. I would soon taste freedom, king of the apartment, master of my own time.

That evening, my loved one left me at home.

"I'll call you when we're done," she said as she unlocked the front door, "you'll come and get me so I don't walk home alone."

"Sure, okay," I replied impatiently, convinced that all of her friends were far quicker door unlockers than she.

The footsteps slowly receded. I locked the door. Blissful silence. I raised my hands in a fist of victory. I. Am. Alone. Free. I can do whatever I want. Anything I ever wanted. The only problem is that everything I ever wanted to do involved someone else doing it with and/or to me.

I was thinking what I should do. I could totally watch porn.

Noooooo, I'm not going to watch porn. I don't need it. I'm content without.

I threw myself on the couch. I flipped through all the TV channels. Nothing of merit to be found. Luckily, though, I was able to do whatever my heart desired. No one could command me. I was free. I got and walked around the living room. I parambulated slowly, my head held high. I chose, of my own free will, to walk in circles around the dining table. Because I could. She will call me when she needs me to rush to her side. "Come to me," she will say unto me. "I miss you," she will whisper through her rubicund lips. "Take me home, I am scared." I checked my phone. No messages. That meant that the wife was having a good time. I was, too.

One stupid TV show ended. I walked over to the closet and chose what I would wear when she called me to come and get her. Her friends would be there. I could put on a white shirt. I'd leave the top two buttons undone, to emphasize my raw masculinity.

She didn't call. For a moment, I was gripped by fear. What if she had a good time...without me? I quickly shook this idea off as an impossibility.

I stood before the mirror. Dressed. I practiced a smile to flash when I stepped into the cafe and her friends turned to me. I would pretend to be happy that they're having a good time, but deep down I hoped they were totally bored. But if they were totally bored, surely she would call me...

A text message arrived near midnight.

"I'm coming alone."

I was in shock. Alone? She didn't want me to come for her. She didn't want her friends to see me. I was deeply affected.

She must have met someone. The waiter? Impossible. There are no good waiters in Slovenia. What if there were no friends at all and the girl's night out was just an excuse? Maybe I should go there and surprise them?

Another text message arrived: "Take a shower."

Ah, now it's clear to me. She didn't want to burden me with retrieving her. She missed me like mad and needed me badly. That could only mean one thing. Good that I didn't watch porn.

I typed my reply: "Showered :)"

She replied: "Warm the bed :)"

I zinged back: "Anything for you ;)"

I lay in bed, warming it frantically. The front door was unlocked. The wife arrived home. I unrolled the blanket just enough to inadvertently show off my bare, mighty thigh. I heard the shower running.

Heeheehee.

She slid slowly into bed, switched off the light and lay beside me. "Thank you for warming the bed for me," she whispered so softly. "Good night, darling."

I was stunned.

"Good night? How's that a good night? Why did you send me to take a shower?"

"So you don't wake me up by doing it in the morning."

She turned away from me.

I should've watched porn.

The Battery Died

It was 8:30am and the banker was late. We had to be downtown to sign some papers.

The wife stayed with me for a while, but then nervously wandered away. "I'm waiting for you in the car," she said impatiently, before she disappeared.

A good half hour later, the papers were signed and my banker and I parted ways. I almost ran to the car. We were really late for each of our next meetings. I leapt into the car. Loud music and warm air rushed to greet me. My beauty was calmly browsing Facebook on her phone. She didn't seem angry. That was a good sign. The last thing I needed this morning was an argument.

"I made myself comfortable," she said with a smile, pointing to the heated seats, the radio and the phone plugged into the charger.

I smiled back and praised her. I adored my wife and I really felt badly about leaving her to wait in the car so long. Now we could finally push off.

I grabbed the steering wheel with my left hand, while the right twisted the key in the ignition. I started the engine.

Tk-tk-tk-tk...tk...tk...

Any driver who has ever started a car with an empty battery will recognize this sound straight away.

"Won't start?" the wife inquired.

"The batter is dead, motherfucker!" I hissed while ever so subtly implying that she was to blame for this state of affairs.

"Not necessarily," she retorted, her face once more buried in Facebook. "Try it again."

Tk--tk--t...k...

"The battery's dead!" I turned to her.

"What are you looking at me for? It's a Hyundai, you can't drain the battery just like that."

Huh?

"Look," I snorted nervously, "you had the ignition on for half an hour. The front and rear lights were on, the radio was so loud that the rust was shaking from the exhaust pipe."

She wasn't convinced. "And now it's my fault? Call your banker and have your car repaired. He was late, not me."

I knew immediately that this was a crisis situation. I thus behaved accordingly. I ordered my wife to call the towing service, because it was her car and her assistance card. A woman in misfortune will be sent aide more swiftly than a man who is furious at his wife.

My dear cooperated and made the call. The conversation went a little something like this.

Wife on the phone: "Hello, our car died."

Me: "Tell him it's the battery."

Wife on the phone: "I don't know what's wrong, it just died, it doesn't want to start."

Me: "Tell him you drained the battery."

Wife (turning to me): "The guy's asking if the engine starts."

Me: "Yes, it starts, but not enough for ignition. It's the battery."

Wife on the phone: "My husband says the engine starts."

Me: "Dammit, bring some jumper cables and we'll be sorted!"

Wife on the phone: "I told him it's not necessarily the battery. God only knows what it is."

Me (foaming at the mouth): "You drained the fucking battery! What are you telling him!?"

Wife on the phone: "Thanks, we're waiting. Hope it's nothing se-rious... Yes, we'll just take it to a Hyundai service center."

She hung up and looked at me. "No problem, they'll be here in ten minutes."

Me: "Where are they coming to meet us?"

Wife: "Here. To the car."

Me: "Which car are they coming in? Did you tell them that cars need special access to reach this lot, otherwise you can't get in?"

Of course I knew she hadn't mentioned it. I was there the whole time. I was the one with foam coming out of my mouth.

"Don't worry, honey. It's a Hyundai. Everything will be fine. Turn on the radio so we can pass the time more quickly."

My eyes rolled into the back of my head.

Ten minutes later, the wife's phone rang. The road assistance guys were on the road, fifty yards from us. They couldn't get any closer because they needed special access to reach us in the parking lot. I ran over to them and asked them to leave their chariot on the roadside and come by foot. They shouldn't concern themselves with traffic wardens.

The assistance guy climbed into our driver's seat and turned the key. Our car started immediately.

"Ah, there you go, not so bad, right?" my wife happily chirped at me. "It's a Hyundai!"

The week passed with my rage slowly cooling. She had the battery running on full blast for half an hour! Every normal human knows that this will drain the battery.

At the end of the week, I drove to volleyball practice. Two hours of hard plays, surrounded by my fellow men, did me a world of good. I even scored a few powerful points and defended a few more. I proudly said goodbye to my team and headed for the car. Even from a distance I saw a pair of headlights like deer's eyes in the parking lot. The headlights of my car.

Tk--tk--tk...

Survival

"Honey, you know you could do that," my wife said to me several times during the show.

"Of course I could," I managed to utter through the clenching of my stomach. The kids on the reality show, Survivor, were desperately clinging to pillars so as not to slip to the muddy ground and thus be expelled from the island. The wife and I watched, while snuggling cozily on our muddless couch.

Every Wednesday, Thursday and Friday night, I listened to this sort of battle hymn to my deification: "You are my Survivor, you would mop up the floor with the competition, you can do it all, you're the best." Now, I'm not foolish enough to oppose a woman's opinion, especially not her sterling opinion of me. So, naturally, I agreed with everything she said.

"Look, honey, this one doesn't even know how to assemble a ladder out of bamboo. You would put it together in a flash and win."

Yes, darling.

"Wow, what I wouldn't give to see you competing there, solving all those puzzles. You're so smart, you're the best."

Of course, darling.

"Look at him, he's been fishing for immunity for thirty days! You, my love, would have had immunity from the first day, alone, without help.

Ug.

I endured these empty compliments and hollow superlatives for a few weeks, but slowly they eroded me. I could no longer bear the false support of my wife's blindness.

"Honey, we need to talk," I said one late night after the show.

"Say it, my savage, my greatest undiscovered Survivor the world has never known."

"You know, these tests they have to do on the show…they're… tough."

"I know that, my love, that's why I'm so proud of you for being able to surmount them all."

"Well, thanks, but I weigh a hundred kilos, you know?"

"Yeah, you'd lose weight on the island and then win."

"That's true, but my muscles are only good enough for volleyball, tennis and splitting firewood. That's about it."

"But you'd get dreamy muscles there, too, you know and then you could do it all and win."

"They don't get anything to eat."

"That's because they're incompetent, honey. Because they don't go into the forest and catch a rabbit and roast it. You would think of doing something like that and have food. You'd be the only one who could."

"I'm not so sure that's the case. You don't see any animals where they are. They can't find any fish even though they're by the sea."

"They couldn't find fish if someone slapped them in the head with a mackerel. You, on the other hand, would lie in wait, somewhere secret, quiet and still, all alone, and then you'd catch them. You would be the only one who could do it.

Truth be told, I did catch one fish once at sea, but that lone act somehow didn't give me confidence in her confidence in me.

"Look, wife, it's not that easy to catch a rabbit."

"I know that, my handsome husband, but once you killed a wasp with your bare hands. You can do anything!"

Oy vey.

Desperate, I made my way to the bathroom. I removed my t-shirt and looked in the mirror. What if the wife were right? What if she saw something in me that I couldn't see myself?

I took a deep breath. I pushed my shoulders forward a little and strained my back. Not bad for someone flying toward fifty. Maybe I was doing my wife a great injustice in not believing her. This body of mine probably really could overcome all those obstacles on that island. These legs could carry me far, provided luck wound my way. This mind of mine, adept at mathematics and overall...

You know what? Maybe the wife was right?

I switched off the bathroom light and climbed into bed brimming with self-confidence. I snuggled up to my bride, hugged her and kissed her warmly.

"What do you want?" she inquired rhetorically.

"Well, you know, my love, we Survivors have a lot of energy to burn at night."

She thought for a moment, then nodded, closed her eyes and said, "You are my Survivor. You can do everything yourself and it'll be even better than when you have to do it with someone else. Good night."

A Bet with the Wife

The Friday night drive to our country house on top of a hill would have passed like any other had not my dearest confidently declared, while we were still in the valley, "There will be no snow up there."

I looked at her in amazement. We've been together long enough for us to know better. But I was not thrown off. I simply replied, firmly and quietly, "There shall be snow, woman."

That's how it kicked off. Statement versus statement until the bet was made.

"What? There'll be snow up there? No way, husband of mine. The sun will be out, there'll be grass, a little rain at the most."

"There shall be snow, my love, and not a little. Perhaps you've forgotten that our house stands at eight-hundred meters above sea level?"

"Perhaps you'll forget my ass! It'll be nice weather up there. I'd bet on it."

Bet on it? My wife, who I looked upon as a great beauty but one meteorologically discordant, would bet with me, a man who practically grew up in the woods?

"You're on," I said. "Let's bet. What are the stakes?"

"Let's first determine what I get if there's no snow up there," replied the family meteorologist. I smelled an opportunity.

"If you win, we'll make wild love tonight."

"You're an idiot," she replied with meteorological accuracy.

"What's wrong with the prize?"

"Nothing, except that we do it practically every day, so it's not a reward."

"Okay, so tonight we'll make love twice."

"Ah, but twice actually means once, then you wake up again eight hours later and do it again. I want a reward that will be mine alone, something special for me."

I honestly didn't care what she chose, because I knew there would be snow up there. But I was happy to make suggestions.

"What about a nice foot massage, my dear?"

"Forget it. You wouldn't know anatomy if you found a foot up your ass. Your idea of where the foot ends is somewhere well above the thighs."

Thus ended my fountain of suggestions that would end to my benefit. For a few moments the blinded opponent thought quietly, then she shouted: "I know! You'll make me a sandwich for dinner!"

A fucking sandwich? The only sandwich I could imagine claiming as a prize was one in which I was the meat and two naked ladies were the bread.

"Can we talk about how I'm going to be rewarded now?" I was in a hurry because we'd started the ascent already.

"Of course we can. I'm guessing it has to do with sex, right?" My babe took a wild stab at it and was correct in her interpretation that it would involve wild stabbing.

"I suppose so. I was thinking if we could finally…"

"Forget it, grizzly bear, we've covered this topic."

"But you picked the sandwich, why can't I pick my prize?"

"You can. As long as it's some type of sandwich."

Very funny.

"And that kind of sandwich isn't an option," she continued, reading my mind. "The only viable ingredients are already inside our refrigerator."

I was slowly growing indifferent as to what reward I would reap.

"Well, you suggest what you'll do to me if it snows," I yielded.

"I'll make you a sandwich," said my doe. She leaned back, satisfied, and added, "with lots of ham and cheese."

What a stupid bet.

It was snowing on our hill. We stopped at the first slope and waited for the plow to clear the road to our house. Or at least to a few hundred meters from our house. Some idiot parked a car in the middle of the road so the plow could go no further. We tramped through the snow and up two more slopes to reach our home. I was carrying two heavy bags and a backpack.

When we entered the house, we knew just what to do. The wife lay on the couch, tired and hungry. Without a word, I set off for the kitchen to make a sandwich.

Two in Bed

I love my wife. I cooked lunch for her. For her, I leapt headfirst into the thorny woods to gather tinder to light the barbecue. I wore a tight-fitting t-shirt because she liked it, even though my chest hair showed through the over-stretched material.

I love my wife, so we sleep in the same bed. The bed is so wide that each of us could log roll twice and still stay on it. We're very happy with the bed.

We used a single, enormous blanket to cover the bed, so we could more comfortably cuddle beneath it. We used to use two smaller blankets, one for each, which is more traditional in this part of the world. Then it was always a confusion: should I slide under hers to facilitate cuddling or should she shimmy under mine? Either way, one blanket was too narrow for us both. This inevitably ended up with me cold and her fully-covered. When I would pull my blanket over me, it would slip off her. Her blanket was never in danger of distancing itself from her spectacular body. She clung to it with a ninja death grip, with the ferocity with which I clung to my subscription to Playboy.

So we went for a single blanket. A giant blanket. Two and a half meters wide. Inside, my loved one was able to wrap up like a hot dog and I had enough slack left to do the same. A pair of warm hot dogs.

But not everything in our bed was a happy ending fairytale. Unfortunately, fairness was required. The bed was one and we were two, which meant some basic math was at play. But let me be clear: I didn't want to yield even a millimeter of my half.

The pre-sleep ritual was the same every night. First, my creeping fingers felt for the seam that ran along the middle of our mattress, marking the precise 50/50 division line. In the darkness, I double-checked to make sure that the seam had not moved, and then ensured that the distance from each of our pillows to this Maginot

Line in the middle was equal. There had to be just enough space between the pillows for me to place my open palm between them. My body, gecko-like, regulates temperature through my hands and feet, so it's important that I sleep without them covered.

There was always the danger that my darling would fall asleep before I was able to get out my protractor and make sure the pillows were evenly spaced. Then I couldn't push the pillow because of her heavy head because the pillow was so soft. So I'd reach around her, grab the other side of the pillow and pull instead, dragging her head away from me and to the appropriate position. If she woke during this process, that was fine, as my motions gave the illusion that I was going in for a kiss, and I'd just whisper that I loved her, which of course I did, and all was well.

Sometimes I couldn't muster the dexterity to pull off this maneuver. The wife would wake halfway through, mutter something incoherent, lift her head off the pillow for a second, and turn to the other side. Since I could predict this sequence of actions, I had to be deft and, just as she raised her head for that second, I'd push the pillow away.

With the pillows each in the right position, I'd check with my other hand how far I was from the edge of the bed. If I was too close, I'd reset the pillows. Both, of course. Symmetry must reign supreme in bed, I've always been taught. Or maybe the word is synergy? Ah well, something that starts with "sin."

Finally, all is in place. The pillows are equally spaced from the edge and from each other and our mutual blanket quotient is sufficient. My love breathes slowly and deeply in sleep. It's nice when the love of my life sleeps so peacefully.

But now I can't sleep. I feel like I am missing my love. I slowly began to push my lightly chilled gecko feet against her. She slinks away from me, toward the edge of the bed. I slowly approach and hug her. Her breathing stops. Like a housefly, she pretends to be dead. I start bouncing around the bed. She still doesn't appear to be breathing. I had to do something.

"Alenka?" I whisper.

"What is it, Kesar?" this wondrous creature burbles.

"Alenka, my love, I'd like too…"

The most beautiful woman on the planet turns to me and strokes my cheek.

"I know exactly what you'd like, big boy," she whispers back.

"You do?" My heart thunders.

"I know, Kesar. The leftover fried chicken is in the fridge. Treat yourself, you can have it all."

Then she re-hot-dogged herself in the blanket and turned her back to me.

That night I was not hungry.

You and Your Salad!

"Honey, did you buy butter?"

"Butter? No, honey. We still have butter in the fridge, enough for us to use this weekend."

"How can I bake cookies if I don't have enough butter?"

"Why didn't you buy it?"

"Me? I should've bought butter for you? I bought everything else!"

I bowed my head. It was instantly clear to me that this was indeed my responsibility. My darling had assisted me with this realization of an absolute truth. So I got into the car and drove to the village store. Along the way, my phone vibrated. A text: could I also get a dozen eggs, as there were only sixteen still in the fridge? Better not to ask. But when I returned from the store, it fired up anyway.

"You were the one who wanted a salad," the wife began, rather calmly, "so wash it."

It occurred to me to counter this queen's gambit with the reposte that I'd been wanting and washing salad for over thirty years, and I did not need such precise instructions.

So I prepared the salad. I tore the lettuce with my bare fingers and threw the shreds into a big bowl. When I'd finished, I put said bowl under the tap, let flow the water, and started to wash the lettuce.

"What are you doing?" it hissed.

"I'm washing the lettuce," I explained to my wife.

"You're breaking it, not washing it!"

"Huh?"

"You're BREAKING it!! Who could eat such lettuce?"

That broke my breaking point.

"I'm breaking the lettuce? I've been doing the same thing for years and so far you've always eaten it. Now all of a sudden you don't like my lettuce because I'm breaking it?"

"I've never liked your lettuce breaking!"

"Goddammit, next time you'll just get a can of chickpeas on a plate!"

"Leave it to me, I'll wash the lettuce. I have to do everything myself!"

That rebroke my already broken breaking point. She had to do everything herself? I even made lunch! I bought three types of cutlets for the wiener schnitzel: veal, pork and chicken, because my fucking wonderful children don't know exactly which meat will suit them, so I breaded some of them straight up, some with shredded coconut mixed in, and some with chopped almonds. I made mashed potatoes and beef noodle soup! She has to do everything, huh?

She rushed at me and began to gently, tenderly wash the lettuce, careful not to injure it any further. My little lettuce-let, I won't let that big, strong man break you any further. A perfect touche occurred to me, and I thrust at her with the query on how she eats the salad without breaking it with her teeth. Does she inhale it like a liquid? Does she even swallow it?

I removed myself from the kitchen, threw on my overcoat and shoes and exited the house. I was about to step onto the grass outside, when I stopped myself.

I didn't dare.

What if I broke it?

Sex as Philanthropy

Evening blanketed the village, its cottages dotted with red and white flashing lights, weaving a fairytale as we drove home. We held hands, listened to the radio, sang softly to each other. A wonderful evening was behind us and a wonderful night ahead. We would take advantage of it. In a few days, I'd have to travel on business.

"Kesar, if you ever cheat on me, you are a dead man," the wife snapped, out of the blue, like a heart attack thundering through a peaceful, clear blue sky. I almost let go of the steering wheel.

"Where did that come from?"

"You know very well. Those two night when you'll be alone, without me for the first time since the wedding, and a bevvy of beautiful maidens around you."

"Come now, what happened to you all of a sudden?"

"Kesar, if you so much as touch a single one of them, you're dead! Just so you know."

Something told me not to play her game. I had to select my strings to strum, my melody, my script. I had to strike back.

"Who says I'll be away only two nights?"

Her eyes popped out of their sockets.

"What do you mean?"

"Well, I don't know which flight I'll manage. If it's too late, I'll leave the day before, if not..."

"Three nights without me? Lucifer's mounds, you're going to be gettin' jiggy with it in great abundance, eh?"

I'd pulled her from her script into mine.

"Isn't it better to get jiggy with multiple jigglers rather than one many times?"

I was tightrope walking and I could only survive if I turned this into a joke.

"Would you like to be killed more than once?" she retorted.

"Well, you can't kill me more than once. Technically speaking." I mocked her empty threat.

"But I can slice you up into tiny noodles before I kill you, Kesar! Don't mess with me!"

You'd think I would stop, but I was incorrigible.

"What if there's a good reason for my behavior?"

"GOOD REASON? What could be a good reason, Dead Man?"

"Look," I began, hoping I didn't run out of slackline. "I'm a good man. I like to help. What if I meet a woman who is unhappy? Who has never had beautiful things happen to her? She has never fallen in love, she has never experienced majestic sex? What if she asks me to show her what majestic sex is? What if she sheds a tear. Shouldn't I come to her aid?"

She thought for a moment. She sighed slowly, caressed my hand as it wrapped the gearshift, leaned over to me so that her lips touched my ear and said, coldly, "I like that you're philanthropically minded, Kesar."

"Really?" My eyes lit up.

"Really. We can add that to your tombstone. 'He was charitable.'"

We arrived home in silence.

The wife knew I wasn't interested in others. She knew that I would quite like to live for a few more years, at least. I had a mortgage to pay off, anyway. But I was planning on renovating the kitchen. I would not allow my plans to fail simply because I'm a philanthropist.

Her Ryan

A hectic week was behind us. We waited for evening to come, so we could throw ourselves onto the bed, exhausted. We lay on our sides, staring at each other. Every now and then we whispered something quietly, more like the end of a conversation than the start of one, with no desire for expansion.

Night swept over our house, the house on the hill in the midst of spruce and pine trees, blanketed in snow so deep that our knees would barely peek over it. We agreed that life was good for us and may this goodness long continue.

I carefully brushed a lock of hair away from my beauty's brow. I moved closer to her and kissed her gently. The kiss she returned to me was not quite as hot as I'd hoped. She looked up and her eyes begged me to fall asleep. They uttered without words that we both know how much we love each other, and we don't need to prove it through physical demonstrations every night. I had a hard time agreeing. I quite like physical demonstrations.

I hugged her to me and whispered that I missed her, that I needed her, that only she could make me feel like a man. We agreed that I was being manipulative. My darling closed her eyes. I knew I had to make the right move in just one more try if I wanted tonight to be crowned by the majesty of physical love.

"Darling," I whispered.

"What?" she barely expelled from those beautiful lips.

"Do you love me?"

"I love you."

"Would you cuddle me a little?"

"Nope."

There went my first idea.

"Alenka."

"WHAT?"

"What if you are completely passive…"

"You are not normal!" she hissed and turned away.

Okay, that idea didn't work, either. I had to think of something that would pump blood to all the right parts of her body, and quickly.

"Dear?"

"Are you serious?" She didn't even turn towards me.

I had no choice. I had to attack with all cannons, emotional and physical.

"I don't excite you anymore," I said with calculated volume.

"Asshole."

"You have a lover!"

"You are fucked up in the head, geezus."

"I won't last forever!"

"Bravo, genius. All women fall for men promising not to last forever."

As always, when I'm pushed into a corner and there's no obvious way out, an idea appears to me that is aglow with light and possibility, one so ingenious that it's worthy of its own category of Nobel Prize.

"You know what hurts most," I said, trying to sound hurt, "if I looked like Ryan Gosling, you'd be all over me right now."

"Oh, at least you've got one thing right, chief."

And with that I saw sex at the end of the tunnel.

"If I were Ryan Gosling," I continued cautiously, "what would you do to me?"

The most beautiful woman in the world finally turned back towards me. Her eyes sparkled and her lips curled into a gentle but triumphant smile. She grabbed me by the neck, pulled me to her. Somehow she stripped and clung to me. Her hands meandered my body, driving me mad. I caught my breath between passionate kisses, tried to follow the rhythm of her body, but then I snapped!

I took her face in both hands and gently, carefully pulled her away from me. She stared back in amazement. But I was boiling inside. I couldn't take it anymore.

"Oh, so you'd do that to Ryan, but not to me when I've been asking nicely all evening?"

I could tell by the look on her face that I'd made a move that would not end well. For me.

"What did you just say?" she hissed.

"You heard it right. Ryan gets the jungle cat, but with me you're the sleeping cat curled up by the fire!"

"I cannot believe it," she said, crossing her arms. "Did I really manage to marry the village idiot?"

"Yes!" I agreed so quickly that I didn't quite realize what I was agreeing with. "I feel hurt. Why aren't you like that when you're with me?" I continued, not knowing why or what I thought I'd get out of it.

"What exactly would you like from me, Kesar? When I'm tired, you're not happy. When I climb on you, you're not happy. What do you want?"

The wall collapsed. Well, Kesar, I thought to myself, what would I really want from my wife? I slowly straightened up, took her hand, and repented. "My love, I want to be your Ryan."

She rolled me onto my back, nibbled me gently on the neck and whispered in my ear, "Then shut up Ryan and let me show you a few tricks."

I fell silent.

Ah, that Ryan. He really knows how to live the high life.

The Disease Called Man

Men suffer from two conditions which are the font of many a problem: lack of sex and a mild cold. The big problem with both, however, is that neither is noticeable beyond the confines of our own little heads. For this reason, we men need to make ourselves look as poorly as possible so that others will see our suffering and take care of, and pity on, us. Then when, a few days later, we rise like a phoenix from the ashes, those around us are astonished by the recovery. They tell us how tough we are, that we will live to be centurions, that nothing can mess with us, not even insidious disease. To be fair, no one can say for sure exactly what we had, but everyone is very sure that they don't want it themselves.

There is something else consistent to these two conditions. If we focus on the latter, the former automatically kicks in. Because the wife doesn't want to catch a cold, long before the Covid pandemic, when sneezes were innocuous.

I recently caught the latter. A cold. In the middle of the week, early in the morning, on my way to the office, it happened. I sneezed. It happened in the hallway, where no one witnessed. I was the only one who knew I sneezed. I, alone.

Once inside the office, I told a colleague that I'd sneezed.

"Bless you," she replied.

"No, no," I said, "it was a proper sneeze, I think I've caught something."

"If you're feeling sick, you should go home," my colleague confirmed. "Those are the rules you set here at the company."

"But if I go home, no one will see that I'm sick."

She smiled in a kindly way at me.

Sometime after noon, I should have sneezed a second time. There was one of those tickly sensations under my nose. Unfortunately I was with my wife and friends on the ground floor of a restaurant and so no one could see. I scrunched up my nose a bit, but nobody noticed. Well, my wife did ask me if I was about to orgasm, but I'm pretty sure she was making fun. If I do, then I sincerely hope that I'll be thinking of her when I do so.

But I didn't sneeze. I explained to all present that I'd already sneezed once today and that I was definitely not well. I did not make it up.

After a whole day of meetings, I felt desperate. Yet no one noticed a thing. My nose wasn't dripping, nor was it red and my appetite was unaffected. At home, my darling made me tea. My wife actually liked it when I got (a little) sick. It didn't matter to her whether the disease was real or imagined. All that mattered was that she had me under complete control. She cared for me. I was helpless, which is synonymous with obedient. This was not my natural state.

We watched TV that evening. I asked the wife to lower the volume.

"You poor thing, is it bothering you?"

No, dear, but I might start sniffling and snoring and sneezing and I want to be sure you'd hear.

We went to bed. She leaned over me and gently stroked my cheeks. She loves to stroke my cheeks.

"You know," she said with a sexy smile, "it would only be right for you to sweat it out."

I immediately agreed.

"I'll be right there," she said, slipping out of the bed.

I quickly stripped naked and pulled the sheet up to my neck. She loves surprises.

She returned to the bedroom.

Carrying hot tea with honey and lemon.

Flirting with a Rose

In my country, we celebrate "Women's Day." I was on a mission to buy six roses, for six ladies. That morning, I slipped into a nearby florist's shop. The friendly florist greeted me with a smile.

"I was expecting you," she said. This caught me by surprise.

"Oh really? How's that?"

"You and your wife stopped by yesterday," she explained, full of energy, "and I heard the lady give you instructions on what to buy."

I swallowed hard and lifted my gaze from the floor. So long, male ego. Welcome, submissive husband.

The florist stood before me.

"She was looking somewhere in this direction when she told you what to buy, right?" She giggled, pointing to vases full of flowers. She was clearly enjoying herself.

"Well," I corrected her, "she wasn't pointing somewhere in this direction, but right there, at those damn red roses."

"Ah-ha!" she exclaimed, approaching the damn red roses. She selected the most beautiful and began to carefully pull them out of the vase.

"The lady said you needed six, right?" she stated rather than asked. "You're lucky to have such a woman by your side. She will tell you everything you have to do, so you'll never make a mistake."

The florist and I clearly had conflicting opinions about what was good for me. I consciously ignored the oxymoron about who should make such decisions.

"Sure," I agreed, lacking the strength to fight a consortium of women. "You're right, it's nice to have a wife like that. Would you please choose a rose with more thorns?"

She laughed playfully. "You're a bundle of fun."

I exited the flower ship with six damn red roses. A young mother who was pushing a baby carriage past the florist smiled at me. I smiled back at her. I didn't want to mess around.

A young couple approached from the opposite direction. The guy was in a collared shirt. He looked like he didn't yet need to shave. The girl beside him had long, dark hair. She looked at me shamelessly and smiled thoroughly until they walked past. The guy didn't notice a thing. I was mad at her on his behalf. He's certainly not allowed to admire other girls when he was with this girl, who incidentally did not look half bad herself.

Two elderly ladies stood at the entrance to a pharmacy, chatting away. I didn't hear the conversation. I was too busy repeating the list of medicines the wife had ordered me to buy. Somehow I wove my way past these guardians at the gate. They smiled in my wake. I know, rude of me, right? I should have asked them to step aside. I was technically third in line. The pharmacist looked at me. She didn't let me out of her sight. She probably recognized me. Or recognized that I was a submissive husband type. The type who only knows how to buy medicines when the wife gives detailed instructions. But her smile didn't fade and I suspected she would try to sell me some un-necessities. When she didn't, I was confused.

Emerging from the pharmacy, I had to snake past the old ladies again. Still smiling. One even winked at me. Maybe I was the very subject of their chitchat? Or this was simply a tick in the facial muscle system of an elderly citizen.

I arrived at the office and handed out the flowers. It was nice to see so many smiling faces.

The conversation among the coworkers drifted here and there until it was time for me to head out for lunch. I put my hands in my pockets and walked out of the office, then downtown.

No one looked at me. No one smiled.

I returned to the florist for a new bouquet. A nice bouquet of colorful, vibrant flowers for the friend we'd arranged to lunch with. I emerged from the flower shop. A Croatian woman was standing in front of a shop window, holding her husband's hand. Our gazes met. She smiled.

The next morning I dressed nicely at home and put on elegant shoes. I grabbed my keys and some coins for a morning coffee. I dropped them into my jacket pocket and put the jacket on, followed by my backpack. Before stepping through the door, I grabbed a colorful, vibrant bouquet of plastic flowers. I wouldn't give it to anyone. I'll just carry it around with me all day. There's no better cure for the male ego than to have unknown girls smile at me on the street.

Neighborhood Sport Bets

Just about every weekend, my neighbor and I sit in front of our country house at the top of the hill in Rakitna, discussing the past and the future and drinking coffee. My darling prepared it for us and even accompanied it with a side order of crepes with chocolate and vanilla ice cream. To stuff us menfolk silly in anticipation of tackling the housework.

Our conversation wound its way to football (by which I, as a European, mean soccer), to Scots and Slovenes, to small players and big coaches. What is right, what's wrong, what's public knowledge and what is concealed? Just before we concluded, my neighbor surprised me.

"Do you bet on sports?"

"Oh, no," I replied, surprised. Why did he even ask me that? I'm not the betting type. At least I don't think of myself as being so. I work. I work a lot. That's how I make a living. I don't do games, lottery, luck. In my head me and betting would make an odd couple.

"And you?" I replied, politely, anticipating an answer in the negative because, as far as I could tell, he was likewise not a gambler. This man had built his house with his own two hands. He worked more than I did.

"Not since last Saturday," he calmly said, before taking a sip of coffee.

"No?"

He set down his cup and laughed. He explained that he places sports bets regularly. Football, handball, hockey. In Europe, in the US, even in Brazil.

"Every week?" I probed.

"Every week."

For a moment I pitied him. He was addicted, I thought, and will lose everything he's worked so hard for. I grew sad but, because I knew nothing about this world, I kept asking. Soon my darling joined the debate.

"Do you ever win anything?"

"Oh, of course, many times," he smiled. "But you know, I bet 50 cents. Sometimes 60 or 70 cents. And I never place bets online, because then you can really get pulled in. Instead I remember the bet number and pull into a gas station and actually place the bet, pay for it, there."

I leaned back in relief. So he was not addicted to gambling, just having some low-key fun.

The eyes of my bride began to glow. The combination of low stakes, potentially high returns and adrenaline stirred her soup. She began drilling our neighbor with questions. What did he bet? She said she had a good nose for winners. Our neighbor laughed.

"Okay, let's take a look. Last week I bet on the Portuguese second division."

"Yeah, yeah, come on, tell me what you bet, and I'll tell you what the result was," she urged impatiently.

"You didn't even know that there was a Portueguese second division until about ten seconds ago," I replied.

"Silence!" hissed the wife, turning back to our neighbor. "Tell!"

"Okay," he said, his smile stretching from ear to ear. "Covilha versus Fafe?"

"Pooh," the wife expelled, "they both have miserable names, of course it was a tie game."

Our neighbor's smile faded a bit. "It was one to one," he said. "How about Leixoes versus Sporting?"

"Huh, Sporting sounds promising and I can't even pronounce the first one. Sporting won."

Now the neighbor's smile was gone. He thanked us for the coffee, stood, took two steps towards his house, then turned to my wife and said, "Madeira versus Famalicao."

"Madeira," my dearest replied almost wearily before retreating to our house.

Our neighbor looked like he'd been hit with a shovel. "She got all three right," he whispered, before sitting back down beside me.

That was when gambling fever hit me. I mean, if my love gets three out of three just based on the club names, we're riding a winner.

"Look," I said, leaning in to the neighbor. "Let me explain how this goes because, you know, if the wife hits it like she did just now, we can each have our own jacuzzi installed by next week."

So we opened up an online betting platform and went through the options.

In the case of AS Melfi vs Akragas (Italian Third League, on the off chance that you're not familiar with them), the neighbor explained to me how to approach these matters in a structured, systematic manner. Above all, logic must prevail.

"Look, you check how they've played so far. Then you check their history. Figure out if they're moving on up or fighting for survival. We check how many goals they score, both at home and away..."

I listened to him with my mouth hanging open, my eyes skittering from one stat line to the next, looking at names of clubs that I'd never heard of.

"And now, we can safely conclude that Melfi will win," my neighbor safely concluded. Then he added a win for Latina to the bet and quickly exited the premises.

I walked into the house, sat down next to my wife and opened the online betting slip. The wife was confident, brimming with knowledge and good vibes. She leaned over and advised me.

"Come on, bet on this match," as she pointed to a random one. "Khimiki will lose at home to Shinnik because Shinnik sounds like a ham in German, Schinken. And I love ham."

I bet on the ham.

At the end of the day, ablaze with visions of newfound wealth, I checked the results.

The wife's ham lost. The neighbor's AS Melfi and Latina, as well. I adjourned to the kitchen to make a conciliatory ham sandwich.

Calorie versus Ego

My dearest stood before the mirror on the first day of spring and measured herself, head to toe.

"Summer's approaching," she whispered softly, turning to check her profile. "Something will have to be done." She glared at her reflection in the mirror. "There's not a swimsuit on the planet that will suit me." She made a hissing sound at the mirror then turned again. "Let alone a bra," she continued, before stepping towards me.

"Kesar, I've made up my mind."

Okay, I thought. Rubicons were there to be crossed.

"Let's go to a spa on a diet."

Oops.

"Let's go on the Slim & Fit program."

Double oops.

I approached the mirror. Some Rubicons are not meant to be crossed. "But sweetheart, look at this physique." I took a deep breath to pronounce my heroic pectorals. I turned sideways. "And look at those lines. At this ass." I turned again. "And the perfect V-shaped torso."

I didn't sense agreement in her eyes. I continued more ardently. "Honey, I wake every day and weigh 96 kilos before breakfast. When I go to sleep, I weigh 97. Every day! I don't want to spoil this well-balanced organism of mine, to be ruined by a program that will throw me out of my daily routine which so optimally maintains both my fitness and Apollonian body."

"You won't, honey. I love you the way you are and I would never want you any different. No, you'll just be accompanying me. As my photographer."

Photographer? Phew. That could work.

Two weeks later, we sat in the office of the nutritionist, the woman on whose words hang the near-term happiness of this husband. She recommended 800 calories, but said we'd get 1200, so it wouldn't be so traumatic. She'd throw in an extra vegetable soup somewhere along the way. I pitied my wife, I really did. With so few calories, I wouldn't be able to get her out of bed. But I was there for moral support, to stand by her side. Or literally off to the side. Maybe a little further still.

"For you, Mr. Kesar, I have planned 1800 calories."

Planned? Mr. Kesar? 1800 calories? The sound roared between my ears and I dizzied. "I'm just her companion. And photographer. I'm neither on the Slim nor the Fit."

"Of course, Mr. Kesar, but you're not going to let the lady endure alone, are you? You're sure to eat with her, because you're there as her companion, right?"

I was cornered. Foul play.

"Anyway, to support her, I'll be staying at the spa with her the whole week. Isn't that enough? Should I be hungry as well?"

"Don't worry, Mr. Kesar, you won't go hungry," she continued calmly. "We're going to have you at 1800 calories a day. For starters."

One thousand eight-hundred calories. Are you screwing with me? That's the number of calories in my Adam's apple. Without realizing it, I'd started stuttering.

"But...but...1800...Mrs. Nutritionist...I burn that by lunchtime..."

"That may well be, Mr. Kesar. If this proves too little, we'll add some the next day." She slowly got up letting us know that our conversation was over.

I turned to my bride for support. I saw tears in her eyes. She was weeping. With laughter.

On a Diet with the Wife: Day One

On the first diet lunch, we sat down directly to a main course. No starter, no dessert, no coffee.

For dessert, we had a walk in the woods. The birds, which had been chirping normally a little earlier, began to honk through the beaks at us. You see, birds subconsciously sense when a hungry predator approaches. A baby in a stroller started crying as we passed. Don't worry, I thought. I'm not that hungry.

After the walk, we went to the sauna. I was naked there. A few women walked past me. I was struck by a barely-controlled desire...to explain to them that my shaft of justice is usually far more imposing, but he's just under stress today. They should come back another time to see him in his proper glory.

On a Diet with the Wife: Day Two

And then came the first weigh-in. Even though I was along for the ride as official photographer, I was banned from taking pictures of the scale. I tried to sneak a snap from behind her back but I was concerned for my physical safety so I backed off.

For breakfast, I selected an omelette and vegetables. One bite and I was already sorry I hadn't ordered it with ham. The nutritionist instructed us to fiercely, ferociously masticate. In public, too. Yes, at least fifteen chews before swallowing. I accepted this advice, minus approximately five chews. Nobody tells this thoroughly experienced gentleman how to masticate.

The nutritionist hunted us down after breakfast, as my beauty and I sat in the cafe nursing our coffees. I subconsciously pushed mine away from me, then blurted out, though no one asked, "It's not mine."

She asked me if I'd been hungry the previous day. I didn't want to admit that I had. She told me that my body would need 2400 calories to function normally. She was putting me on a weight loss program with 1800. She pointed at my tummy. I made a mental note to only speak with her, in the future, while standing up, flagpole straight.

After coffee I needed some tender loving care, but I didn't know if I had enough calories to engage in said activity. I started browsing professional literature and learned that a half hour of sex burns around 200 calories. This required a bit of recalculation based on the actual probable duration of sex. What a great deal! I'd burn a good 20 calories!

The enthusiasm was short lived due to the unfortunate equation that sex always required a second person (at least). My wife did not feel like burning 20 calories. She said that she was already in a caloric deficit. I suggested we first invest in caloric credit, preferably in the form of cake. A sacrifice for her loving husband. I grew concerned for my physical safety so I backed off.

The clock strikes 11.

It's been raining all morning. The outdoor pool is empty. We burn 700 calories in an hour of swimming. I am willing to invest 100 calories into sport. That's eight minutes of swimming. Ah, I can't be bothered to get out of my horizontal position on the hotel room couch for just eight minutes of swimming.

The clock strikes 2.

I sit in the room and gaze longingly out the window. It's still raining and the pool is still empty. We just returned from lunch. Stuffed tomatoes and beef. My stomach rumbles, objecting. The wife falls asleep. A snack eyes me from the table. 180 grams of probiotic yogurt and a baby's fistful of hazelnuts. As designated photographer, I would take a photo of said snack, but I don't have a macro lens with me.

The clock strikes 6.

I go out to the pool, though it continues to rain heavily. I figure this is a good guarantee that the pool will be empty. I feel wonderful. I swim ten lengths without a pause. That's 120 meters. Eight minutes. My stomach roars. Hotel staff, suddenly convinced that a storm bears down on us, rush to the terrace to put away metal chairs and tables.

Back in the room, I wait for the wife on the couch. First dinner, then Champions League football. I inadvertently touch her bare knee with my hand. My wife muttered that such behavior could be construed as assault because she hadn't the calories to defend herself. I didn't know what she was talking about. Then I was confused: was this a warning or an invitation? I grew concerned for my physical safety so I backed off.

The clock strikes 7:45.

We sit at dinner. Immediately after, we ask the waiter for an evening snack: yogurt and crackers. We head back up to the room and lay on the couch. I want to close my eyes, but I can't. Too few calories.

On a Diet with the Wife: Day Three

The clock indicates 8:20.

There's a saying around these parts: the donkey didn't wander onto the ice twice. Think about it.

For breakfast, I order prosciutto and bread and cheese spread with horseradish. The plate arrives: three pieces of bread, four miniature slices of prosciutto. This meant that only half the bread was draped with meat. I coated the rest with the spread. Very thin. Still, half the bread was naked. I sprinkled carrots and zucchini slices over the rest.

For my morning snack, I eat pineapple and grapes.

I eat said snack on the stairs on the way from the breakfast room to our room. With hungry eyes, I wait for my love to return from a cardiocross class. Maybe she won't be hungry and will give me her snack?

The clock indicates 11.

My sweety returns from cardiocross. She eats her snack and, on top of it, my yogurt, which I'd been saving as emergency rations. The relationship between the photographer and the client deteriorates sharply.

The clock indicates 12:20.

The sun peeks over the horizon: our first dessert!

The wife orders me to take a picture of it while she eats. I take many photos, from many angles. While doing so, as a defensive measure, I move my dessert to another table. When she sees me do this, for some reason she no longer wants me to take pictures.

The clock indicates 2.

I had to pop down to Ljubljana. I enter my apartment to change. My mother-in-law, temporarily staying at our place, is cooking lunch. I don't eat it. I am an idiot. It seems I've forgotten that I'm just the photographer.

2:02

Mother-in-law: "Have you lost weight?"

Me: (silence)

2:04

Mother-in-law: "Your jeans are slipping down and your ass is showing."

Me: (silence)

2:06

Mother-in-law: "Pull up your jeans and tighten your belt."

Me: (pulling up my jeans and tightening up my belt)

2:08

Mother-in-law: "That's better. But you still look too skinny."

Me: (silence, interrupted only by the rumble of my stomach)

The clock indicates 7pm.

I return to the spa to serve out the remainder of my sentence. My wife and I sit down for dinner. While I was gone, my darling spoke with the nutritionist. Apparently she stated that a man like me burns 1800 calories a day if he engages in intellectual labor.

Dinner is served.

I'm intellectually furious.

On a Diet with the Wife: Day Four

The Devil has a sense of humor. I've lost enough weight to require my belt to be buckled one hole tighter than before. And all I did was eat and take photos. On the fourth day, I wasn't hungry at all. I even skipped yogurt and the late morning soup. The staff and other guests complimented me, saying I looked better. But the relationship between photographer and client remained tense. My dearest suggested on more than one occasion that I was behaving like a real photographer, instructing her on how to move. Shift this way, there's a shadow over your face! Sit further forward! Suck that belly in! Don't move or it'll be blurry! You had to blink right then!?

This beauteous creature suggested a practical approach to solve this problem. Let the photographer get jiggy with his subject. This would result in better chemistry between them and a better final product.

I told her that I would duly consider the proposal. Until such time as a decision had been made, she should continue to work as I dictated.

The icing on the cake was that my love told me, in no uncertain terms, not to go to water aerobics class with her. I hadn't offered. I also didn't inquire as to why I was banned from doing so. She explained anyway. There was a young, slender, beautiful Russian woman in the group. I should not come so I would not be tempted. She seemed to think that, were I to activate my humble brain and bring my body nearer to another woman engaged in possibly sexy motions, I would collapse from lack of oxygen.

Without meaning to, I envisioned approaching the Russian woman and falling unconscious in front of her. Do Russians know that those who faint are best resuscitated through mouth-to-mouth respiration?

On a Diet with the Wife: Day Five

Captain's Log, Day Five, 8am.

My fifth day dieting. For the third day in a row, I order prosciutto and three pieces of bread for breakfast. It was the option that imbued my fragile body with the most power. We get a pear for a mid-morning snack. I feel strong.

9am.

The biggest investment of the day was expended during water aerobics. The wife asked me to go along. It took place in the adjoining, outdoor pool. I was there to support her. My love, my beauty. I would do anything for her.

9:10am.

I've completed six lengths of the outdoor pool. About 70 meters. Freestyle. Legs working full blast. I couldn't go any further. On my way out of the pool, my knees hurt. I feel nauseous and dizzy.

"Okay, old man," I think to myself, "maybe, just maybe, you're eating too little to perform as a proper photographer."

10am.

I'm seated in the cafe. I drink coffee and a pint of mineral water. A waitress named Lili takes pity on me. She points to my trousers and comments, "That's where you'll see the most significant loss."

How did she know?

11:50am.

The wife and I are seated with the nutritionist. We tell each other everything. Lots of very nice things, as well as something or other about calories. We spend the last five minutes of the meeting on the topic of me. Mrs. Nutritionist calculates how many calories I need to intake to sustain my body through its daily activities. She estimates 3950 calories. The wife laughs out loud. A moment later, she feels sorry for me. Good. I'll take advantage of the pity tonight before bed.

12:30pm.

We emerge from the office. The nutritionist has raised my daily calorie intake from 1800 to 2400. At the same time, she asks us to give her a few minutes to transfer the numbers to the kitchen, so they can be put into effect by lunchtime. A few minutes? What are we supposed to do for a few minutes?

12:31pm.

The wife takes my hand and drags me to the spa. We stop in front of the scales.

"Step up," she orders.

I step up. I look around. Damn. Somewhere en route I seem to have lost two kilos (4.4 pounds).

1pm.

Lunch.

The wife is given two veal cutlets. I have three. For the first time since we arrived at this spa, I feel full.

1:40pm.

I sit in the cafe again. Coffee and mineral water. My stomach feels full. I feel guilty for feeling full. One should suffer, right?

Lili the waitress smiles at me. I don't know why. My veal cutlet couldn't have arrived at my trousers so quickly.

6pm.

I ask the personal trainer if he can teach me to swim butterfly in half an hour. "Can we do it that quickly?" I ask.

"Sure, if you have any talent," he replies.

6:30pm.

I have no talent.

6:40pm.

I sit in the cafe and drink my third coffee. And third pint of mineral water. Lili has gone home. I look down at my trousers. Something moved in there. Damn, maybe it's already showing?

On a Diet with the Wife: Last Day

8am.

Just before breakfast, I step naked out of the bathroom and head for the couch, where my clothes await me. I step past the closet mirror, then back up. I stare into the mirror. I can't believe it. The tummy is gone. The contours of muscles are drawn onto my thighs. What a tight ass I have! The whole body is upright. I summon my dearest. "Come on, honey, you have to see this!"

Turns out she doesn't have time. She's too busy looking at herself in the bathroom mirror.

9:10am.

I'm standing at the edge of the pool. My legs did not resemble a butterfly's yesterday. I visualized how I was supposed to move all evening. It wasn't until this morning that the movement came together for me. Now I'm standing there, ready to do the exercises that the swimming coach showed me.

I step towards the round pillar next to the pool. I stop half a foot-length from the pillar. I place my hands by my sides and lean slowly forward, my chest and head against the pillar. While I am trying to assume the correct swimming position, an objective observer would likely think that I am thoroughly under the influence of alcohol. I slowly lean my abdomen and hips against the pillar, moving my head and chest up and away from it. I move like a dolphin. When I reach my knees, I lean my chest and head against the pillar again. I perform a body wave, as instructed.

The pool has suddenly gone quiet. I feel the gaze of a bevy of babes upon me.

Dammit! I'd forgotten the words of wisdom of the swimming coach: don't practice this move in public or you'll look like a worm trying to make love to a pillar.

9:20am.

You can keep your amorous worms. I swam butterfly dolphin-style underwater!

9:50am.

Tired from a half-hour of dolphin dives, I stroll around the spa. I couldn't find anyone I knew to whom I could brag. This 47-year-old dog had learned a new trick. My dearest wasn't available yet, as she engaged in her own exercise program. Disappointed, I head back to the room.

11am.

I don't hear the door as it opens. The wife catches me looking like a worm trying to make love to our hotel room wall.

Doctor's Orders

I slowly crawled out of bed and moved from the bedroom to the living room. I walked over to my wife and pointed to my throat.

"Something is scratching in there," I whispered.

My darling, who had something called purulent angina a week ago and is now Mistress of Health Care, saw in my plea a chance to save me.

"Come here, lie down on the couch, open your mouth and stick out your tongue," she ordered, as she reached for her phone. She turned on the flashlight feature, aimed it at my throat and examined.

"It might be angina," she concluded, switching off the light. "Call your doctor and say that you'd like to come in straight away. No time to wait, with the weekend approaching."

Before she'd finished her statement, her daughter shoved a school notebook in front of her and showed her parental instructions.

"Honey, you know Mommy can't see well up close." She smiled at her daughter and sent her hunting for her glasses.

"Wait a minute," I complained. "How do you know I have angina if you can't see up close?"

"Your throat is scratchy. I just got over angina and a few days ago you wanted to kiss passionately, despite my warning that you were the one who was going to be fucked..."

A reasonable argument. I called the doctor and made an "urgent" appointment. Possibly angina, I said. Maybe more than angina.

I snarfed down my breakfast and hurried to the clinic. A substitute doctor invited me in.

"Sit down," he said, pointing to the chair. "What seems to be the trouble?"

"I have angina," I self-diagnosed, then leaned back proudly.

I'd just passed the baton to the doctor and was in his hands. It was up to him to save me from the grip of disease.

"How do you feel?" the doctor asked, setting up a lamp to look in my throat. A good deal more professional than the old cell phone flashlight app approach. This gave me an idea of what to buy for my darling for her next birthday.

"I feel great," I replied.

"Fever?"

"Not a chance!"

"Open your mouth and stick out your tongue." That's the second time today someone asked that of me. He illuminated my insides, switched off the light, smiled, nodded and sat back in his chair. He turned on his computer and began to type. When he hit "enter" he turned to me.

"Well, we're done," he said with a broader smile.

"Great." I was pleased. "Do I get a prescription for antibiotics from the nurse?"

"You don't get anything. That's it," he replied, still smiling.

"But my wife got antibiotics. Why don't I get antibiotics?"

The doctor slid up to me in his chair, patted me encouragingly on the shoulder and said, "You don't have angina."

"Why don't I have angina?"

"You can't have angina."

One of us wasn't following.

"I...I can't have it?" I stammered. "But my wife told me..."

"No, I'm afraid you can't."

"Why not, Mr. Doctor?"

"Because you have no tonsils."

Fair enough.

A Visit with the Boxer, Dejan Zavec

The world's most beautiful woman stepped before me.

"Gaze upon me, Kesar!"

I looked at her. A long way down. Geez, she's tiny when she stands so close to me. I could break my neck craning down to look at her. And given that she called me by my surname, I had the feeling that I was in for a long neck ache.

"Don't even think about it, Kesar," she retorted.

"Don't even think about what, my gilded heart?"

I tried to remain calm while subtly stepping back and a little to the right. I saw myself in the mirror again, the largest one we had in our apartment. Not bad for my age, I thought. Tight jeans, lowered just enough to reveal a tasteful glimpse of my undies, barefoot, topless. Combining full lungs and flexed back muscles, I looked fifteen years younger. And dangerous as a mothafucka.

"We're going to visit world welterweight boxing champ, Jan Zaveck," said my bride, determined not to be tempted by my beauty. "Don't make an ass of yourself. Or of me!"

An ass? Moi? Her? The love of my life? Not for all the tea in China.

"Kesar!"

The sound of my name reverberated through our apartment. It's unwise to mess with my tigress when she stands firm before me.

"My love, all will be well. I shall not embarrass you. I will be there to be seen, not heard."

"Promise?"

"I promise."

She didn't budge. I suppose I was insufficiently convincing.

"You won't mention that you've taken up boxing?"

This surprised me. Why shouldn't I tell him that? As Slovenia's most successful and famous boxer, that could bring us closer.

"Well," I objected eloquently.

"Well nothing," she interrupted. "Please don't tell him that. Probably everyone who has ever tried boxing tells him that. But you remember the famous Slovenian basketball player, Jure Zdovc, who we met at that wedding? When one drunk guy cornered him and explained how to shoot a basket?"

Heehee, yup, I remember that. One of the Yugoslav basketball legends, a pleasant man who had been boxed out by an enthusiastic wedding guest showing him how to correct his jump shot.

I understood. My wife was right.

"I understand, my love. I shall not mention that I ever trained in boxing."

My dearest nodded contentedly. And then continued.

"You won't mention that you have a punching bag in the garage?"

"I can't mention that either? But you bought it for me!"

"Do you know how many people have a punching bag? Everyone who has it and has ever met Jan Zaveck has mentioned it to him! He has more of them than you do, so why should he be interested in your punching bag?"

There was some logic to this, I admitted. I promised that I wouldn't mention my punching bag.

"And don't mention that you trained with that MMA fighter, Chorchyp, because he will think that you are bragging and you will look pathetic."

This was getting to be a bit much.

"Should I remain mute? Is it bad that I know a little bit about boxing?"

My wife almost fell over.

"Keep your observations and quotes to yourself, okay? Deal? And can you stop looking at yourself in the mirror!?"

With reluctance, I turned away from the reflection of my youthful body and stared into her eyes.

"Alenka, I promise that I will not mention boxing or Chorchyp or my bag or even that I write. I will be there as your chauffeur and bodyguard. I shall simply stand beside you. Whatever you want."

My wife hugged and kissed me.

"Thank you, my love. I'm proud of you."

Two hours later, we were parked in front of Jan's gym. We headed up to the first floor and into his office. Jan saw us, got up from behind the table and headed toward us with a broad smile. Handshake strong and confident. Jan's was, too.

"Want to take a look at the workout space?" he asked.

I made not a sound. I'd promised my wife. I just nodded and half-smiled. Not too much. Just enough to express interest.

We entered the gym. My eyes misted over. My legs went numb. My breathing paused. It was the most beautiful gym I had ever seen. The punching bags hung, side by side, to my right. The boxing ring, a real, proper boxing ring, shone at the far end of the room. I walked over to one of the bags. It looked to me like it had swallowed a donut. I stroked it. Sorry, darling. I love you most in the world. But a promise is a promise...

I turned to the former world champion, approached him, quite close, so close that I nearly strained my neck looking down at him. Geez, how many people in this world are short?

"A bag for uppercuts..." I muttered, barely coherently.

Jan laughed and nodded. "I see you know your boxing."

I explained everything to him. That I trained, that Chprchyp, the famous MMA fighter himself trained me, that I have a punching bag in the garage, that I practice during the weekend... I was focused, light on my feet, floating like a butterfly. I didn't even slow down when I caught my sweetheart out of the corner of my eye, hiding behind the donut bag out of shame...her eyes boring into me, stinging like a bee.

Someone Has to Keep Their Eyes on the Road

That renowned lover of tall, dark, handsome men--aka, my wife--prepared a bottle of water for the whole family to enjoy on our drive to the seaside. She asked if we could stop at a gas station to grab some coffee, adding, "you never know when history repeats itself. Remember last year's trip."

Before we'd driven another five kilometers, my darling popped open the bottle and took two sips of water.

"Will you?" she offered.

"I will," I replied, reaching out my hand to her.

As long as we've known each other, the queen of my dreams has been tap dancing on my nerves when it comes to the vehicular consumption of food and beverage. I somehow cannot explain to her that I, as the driver at the moment, am the one looking at the road and she, as the passenger otherwise unencumbered by the task of keeping the car on said road, should place food and beverage into my hand so that I do not have to grasp blindly for them.

No, her system differs from what I would prefer. I must take my eyes off the road to search for the proffered sandwich, which she flits around my head. My female co-driver keeps her eyes locked on the road while I reach for the snack. Meanwhile, she keeps warning me to watch where I'm going because I'm about to hit the curb!

She once stabbed me in the eye with a slice of bread smeared with pate.

"Someone has to look at the road," she explained in a hiss.

"Yes, and that someone is me. I'm driving!"

"Obviously not very well if I have to look at the road to keep you from driving off of it!"

In short, this was a game I could not win. So once, out of sheer naughtiness, I decided to really look at the road. I asked her to give me a sip of water. I held out my hand like those LEGO figure, my hand in a caricature plastic crab grip, ready for a bottle to be clicked into place. My queen untwisted the lid and extended the bottle towards me, but of course she did not click it into place but held it a few inches away from my hand, because she was too busy looking at the road. So we drove like that for about a kilometer, me with my outstretched hand, waiting for my beverage, the wife with her hand outstretching the beverage to me. Separated by inches.

"Are you fucking with me!?" she shouted.

I started laughing. "I'm not fucking with you. I just want you to put the bottle in my hand. We can't both look at the road."

She closed the bottle, unsipped, and placed it in the beverage holder between our seats.

"Take a drink yourself when you're thirsty. Nobody fucks with me!"

That was last year. This year, on our way to our much-deserved holiday, a few kilometers after departing, I asked her for a sip of water. My dearest opened the bottle, looked at the road, and placed the bottle not into but upon my hand. She thought I'd grabbed the bottle. I had not. She let go.

"Ah!"

I shrugged as a bottle full of water spilled upon me and soaked my trousers. It was like an elephant peeing on me.

"Why didn't you take the bottle?" That was a question I hadn't expected.

"Me? Take it? Why did you let it go?"

"Because you should have taken it and you didn't! Good thing I was looking at the road, otherwise we would have crashed!"

From that point on, she was the driver and I was her waterboy.

Our New Neighbors

One fine day on vacation, the folks in the mobile home adjacent to ours at the holiday resort were packing up to head home. We hadn't exactly met our neighbors. The father was silent at all times, and perhaps this is why the little child was crying and shrieking from morning until evening, every day. The language with which these parents soothed their sobbing child was not dissimilar to someone gargling a shot of Jagermeister. Dutch. The mother was cute and shapely. She greeted me once during the week and never again. I don't know why I resented her. I'm sure that my smile can heal.

An hour before their departure, a white car with a Dutch license plate wound its way up to their mobile home and they loaded their belongings into it. The noisy child was packed in first, to quench his protestations. A few minutes before they set out, the father approached us and offered us "ice cream and cevapcici, so it doesn't go to waste." He said this to us Slovenes in Dutch-accented Croatian. I was impressed.

That evening, my tanned blonde and I sat upon the terrace of our mobile home and wagered on the nationality of our future neighbors.

"Germans, totally," said the owner of the most beautiful curves in the family.

"You sure about that?"

"I'm sure about that. The wife will be buxom and tall, the husband smaller and quieter."

I giggled to myself.

"They will have two daughters, one a teenager."

"Wow, my minx, you're clairvoyant. What else?" I was having fun. In my head, the new neighbors would be four girls here for a bachelorette party, ready for all the adventures this world has to offer.

"Of course," the center of my solar system continued, "they will bring the bride's mother along."

I slowly stood, stretched and confided my own opinion as to who our new neighbors would be. The wife cackled enthusiastically.

"Yes, of course, four girls, because young girls go to mobile homes on their own!"

I was sorry I'd told her what I was thinking. I hadn't laughed at her when she'd theorized about Germans and their mother-in-law. We went to sleep in silence.

The next day, as we sat down to lunch, the manager of the resort walked past us, accompanied by an affluent-looking lady of my age, her mother and two daughters, one of whom was a teenager. They walked straight into the adjoining mobile home. The fork fell out of my hands.

"Here," said the manager. "Ich hoffe dass Sie einen angenehmen Urlaub haben." Or some sort of generic happy holiday wishes to that effect.

"Danke sehr," thanked the buxom mother, then hugging her mother.

My wife and I locked eyes. Alenka smiled slightly.

"This proves nothing. Yet," I stated, comforting myself. "Maybe German is their only shared language. And the father will certainly look like Paul Bunyan. A woman like that can't be paired with a quiet, small man. And here he comes now."

A car with a German license plate pulled up in front of the mobile home. My beauty waited with baited breath. I waited with a weighted breath.

Out of the car stepped a man. Small and quiet. He greeted his copious wife with a small, quiet greeting. He greeted us, too, in a manner that could best be described as small and quiet. We returned his greeting.

The joy of my life rose and hugged me from behind.

"Well, who's always right, honeybunch?" she whispered in my ear, before heading into the house to get some hard liquor.

With Croatian travarica liquor and coffee on the table, we sat beside our neighbors as they carried their luggage from the car to the house. When their car was empty, and their terrace filled, the lady, whom we quickly realized was the benevolent dictator of the family, opened a nice suitcase, pulled out a tablecloth, and draped it over their table. My beloved's jaw dropped.

"Don't fuck with me," she exhaled. "They brought their own tablecloth!"

I sipped the travarica. So what if they have a tablecloth? We have three tablecloths at home.

"Kesar, next summer we're bringing our own tablecloth. Write that down! See how cozy their terrace looks thanks to that tablecloth?"

I looked at the terrace. Then at the tablecloth. Then at the terrace with the tablecloth. It was a tablecloth. Nothing special.

The mother now pulled out six soft chair cushions from the same nice suitcase. They matched the color of the tablecloth.

"Kesar!"

She squeezed my fingers bloodless. "Why don't we have that!?"

"Leave me alone, woman, how am I supposed to know there won't be pillows on the chairs on our rental?"

"Well, they knew!"

This was all highly suspicious. Something fishy was afoot. The lady reached into the suitcase again and now emerged with two long pillows for the loungers on the terrace. My queen's eyes bugged out.

"Alenka, don't fuck with me, they're clearly not here for the first time. How else would they know that their rental comes with two loungers--and they brought pillows that are just the right dimensions?" I was squealing in my own defense, knowing that I had not thought to ask our travel agent questions along these lines.

"It doesn't matter, sweetheart. It doesn't matter," my better half whispered. "You just observe and take notes."

The lady dipped in a few more times and out came a ring of cooked shrimp for dipping into various sauces. We didn't have this. Or various sauces. Then a folding grill. We were grill-less. We were also bereft of the many meters of rope that the two daughters of the family now stretched around the terrace, over which they threw bedspreads which inconveniently, for us, obscured the viewing pleasure of their curious neighbors. The father pulled out a tape measure, found the perfectly spaced trees adjacent to their terrace, and hung a hammock between them. Grandma hung mosquito nets and placed candles on the table. Then the whole family strung Christmas lights around the terrace.

Satisfied with their work, they congratulated each other. The mother reached back into the magic suitcase and out came five pairs of slippers. Each family member took their pair and entered the house.

That night, we each lay on our side of the bed and mentally composed a list of what to bring next year.

The next morning we finally met the new neighbors. We were pleased to meet them and they were pleased to meet us. We looked normal, they said. Thank goodness, because they didn't always have that luck. Most of their past neighbors didn't want to talk to them at all.

"How many times have you been here?" I inquired.

"This is our sixth year in the same house."

The wife and I met eyes. "No wonder they have such precise supplies with them," I whispered to the conqueror of my heart.

We learned a lot from the Germans.

For example, the fact that mobile homes at this resort are more expensive this year than last. That you have to pay for parking.

That a pizza outside of camp costs 40 kuna, while inside camp the same pizza is 85 kuna. The first row of mobile homes by the sea cost 210 Euros per night. They got their house of 170 Euros per night just like ours. It was too pricey for them so they found a similar resort just a few kilometers away for 130 Euros a night.

A few hours later, my darling and I were back at our table, more travarica and coffee at the ready. A slender, tall, long-haired blonde with two young daughters strolled past us. She stood beside a tree a few paces away from our mobile home. A black minivan slowly drove toward her. I couldn't make out the license plate, but the four bikes hanging off the back told me all I needed to know. Dammit. Slovenians.

It's one thing to have cool bikes with you. It's another to have to also employ your wife to direct his driving so he doesn't back into a tree.

Of course, a Ljubljana license plate. My one true love nodded towards the blonde. "I'm not like that, am I?"

"No, honey, you're not. You wouldn't have gotten out of the car. You would've directed proceedings from the passenger's seat."

It happened that we headed off to the beach just as the new neighbors from Ljubljana did. Their children immediately began to play with ours and seemed to get along very well. Soon after this first round of play, our little worker bees asked, "Can we go and visit them in the afternoon, too?"

Evening came and the wife and I went to visit our fellow countrymen. We spotted their mobile home from a distance. My beloved took my hand and stopped me.

"Look how beautiful the lights are," she sighed. "They have a fence around their terrace, Kesar. We don't have a fence around our terrace. Next year, demand a fence around the terrace."

I nodded. Meanwhile, I suggested that they probably paid through the nose for their mobile home. At least 200 Euros a night, and it wasn't even close to the sea.

We mounted their terrace. The chairs were not as plastic as ours. Theirs were wooden with a brightly-colored lattice of fabric stretched across them. Their table was not a fused plank of plastic, like ours. Theirs was made of teak, or something teak-ish. The sort of material that is used on yachts. Their toilet was spectacular. My angel told me this after she had been obliged to use the facilities urgently. She added that our toilet back home wasn't this nice. And that I should take notes on it.

"What should I note?"

"A nicer evening for next year."

The beautiful wife and pleasant husband placed wine glasses on the table. My dearest pulled a phone from her pocket and took a photo of them. The glasses, not the husband and wife.

"You will attach a photo to the list for next year, Kesar, with the following caption: 'nicer glasses.'"

I didn't complain. I mentioned to her, again, that all this luxury probably cost a lot. At least 190 Euros a night. I felt like she didn't believe me, so I shifted up a gear.

"May I ask how much you are paying for this noble mobile house?" I inquired.

"You won't believe it," they replied in enthusiastic tandem, smiles broadening. "We got a special price. 128 Euros a night."

We slumped back to our humble mobile home. We slowly climbed into bed, each on our own side. My goddess pushed the list for next year into my hands.

"Write, Kesar," she commanded. "Write '120 Euros a night.'"

"120? But they paid 128."

"Write 120, Kesar. We have to win."

I'm Not Allowed Alone on the Beach in My Mini Swimsuit

The phenomenon of swimsuits on the beach follows the same routine every year. I need them three weeks of the year, then they hibernate somewhere in my home and I don't rouse them again until the next summer, shortly before our annual seaside holiday. Seeing as I am as orderly as my wife and children permit me to be, I find my swimsuit sound asleep in the same drawer as always, without giving it much thought, let alone careful inspection. I throw it into my suitcase and that's that. This year, too, I thought that was that. I placed my two favorite swimsuits in my suitcase. After a few days at the seaside, I would be left without either. Turns out that isn't always that.

Regarding the first pair, may they rest in peace, it was an issue of thinness of fabric. On the second day of our holiday it came to my attention that the material on my ass was so thin that it left nothing to the imagination. The elastic around the waist had loosened. This was in part the fruits of my having lost some weight--a whole belt loop--since the previous summer vacation, but also a sign of the many years this pair had spent in service to me. I think I bought them ten years ago, when tight-fitting spandex numbers were still (sort of) in fashion (I live in Europe, remember). The advantage of these swimsuits was that I was able to wear them at nudist beaches with the nudists none the wiser. The downside was that I had to keep pulling them back up each time a rogue wave threatened to turn any beach into a nudist beach. Their tendency to escape my body meant that they were only really suitable for cannonball jumps--definitely not for dolphin dives.

The "newer" swimsuits had gone loose on the side seam and my right thigh was clearly visible. It was only seven years old. I mean, the string was still in place, so the elastic was doing its job. It just had added air conditioning. This pair was fine for dolphin-style diving and bathing, provided water covered me above the waist.

Or so I thought. It didn't take long for my blue-footed booby to lose her temper.

"Kesar, let's go to the store for a new swimsuit. My man can't walk around the beach like that! What will people say about me?"

She was right. If the stitching loosened any more, I'd be the only one on the beach with a split up to my ass. This I could not permit. Or rather, my wife could not permit it.

At the entrance to the store, my beauty paused and nodded towards the cash register. "Let's hustle, slim." She sent me into the fray amidst the shelves of spandex. "Buy yourself a new swimsuit. You deserve it. Everyone else on the beach deserves it. Especially me."

With my head bowed, I entered the store. I looked around. There was no one anywhere. Only a young, well-kept cashier chatting with her young, well-kept friend. Great, I thought, just the two play-by-play commentators I need, as an old man hunting for a modern swimsuit. I approached them.

"Sorry, I'm looking to get myself a new swimsuit. Just the bottoms." This was my attempt at humor. They didn't "get" it." One of them even turned away. I looked towards my wife, who was standing in front of the door like a prison guard, as if afraid I would bolt, if given the chance. She gave me the thumbs-up. Back into battle, my stallion, I'm sure she thought.

The cashier pointed to a display stand.

"There," she said, eloquently. Then she continued to chat with her friend and forgot about me.

I approached the shiny metallic pole, like a tinselled Christmas tree draped in a few miserable black swimsuits, some boxer shorts style, and a light blue extra mini tighty-whities number. The latter pair I wouldn't wear for all the tea in China. They barely covered the front and the back was more ass than swimsuit. Michael Phelps wore larger suits at the Olympics. I quickly averted my eyes.

The black boxer shorts style was a possibility. I held them up triumphantly to my wife, who was still physically blocking the exit with her body. She shook her head. Not good enough.

"You already have a pair like that," she snapped, "choose something better." I was pretty sure I didn't, otherwise why would I need to go shopping for a new swimsuit, but such a parlay would have been unwise. On the other hand, I didn't know how to tell her that this seemed to be the best of the limited options here. She must have read my mind, because she followed up by saying, "And don't come back without a swimsuit."

I shan't my darling, my elegant porpoise of love, my goldfish. I returned the boxers to the stand. All that was left were the simple black suits and the sinful light blue minis. I took the minis off the stand.

It was as if some silent alarm had sounded. The cashier and friend, who'd happily ignored me before, now turned their heads towards me with looks of horror and denial in their eyes. They shook their heads instinctually, dissuading this old man from embarrassing himself and disgusting them. I held the mini up to my bride all the same.

She craned her neck up and forward and opened her mouth in surprise. An enormous smile slowly spread over her face. She raised both thumbs high and shouted across the store, "Kesar, that is the sexiest pair I've ever seen. Purchase! Purchase immediately!"

Embarrassed, I walked over to the cash register and placed the sliver of fabric on the counter. The cashier nodded to her friend who was making her escape from the trainwreck taking place before her. I pulled out my credit card, grabbed the swimsuit and walked out the door.

The wife suddenly became the world's most affectionate woman, showering me with kisses and hugs and heavily breathing: "The moment we get to the house, we go to the beach!"

I stood in front of the mirror at our rental home. I was wearing the world's smallest mini swimsuit, in a lovely light blue. I barely climbed into it without bodily injury.

The, um, pouch was just the right size for nothing to peek out of it, while also accentuating every detail and contour of that which it did not overtly reveal.

"I can't go to the beach like this!" I nearly cried to my wife. "Look upon me. I look like I want to be a teenager, but then look at my legs!"

My legs were really a mess. The few days of holiday had been enough for me to pick up a tan, but only as far as the boxer style swimsuit had covered. Now that I was wearing tighty-whitie minis, the male equivalent of those thongs worn by sumo wrestlers, my milky thighs made me look like I was wearing a pair of white shorts underneath my blue bathing suit.

"No one's looking there," the queen of my life assured me. "Everyone will be looking at your junk up front."

What could I do? My angel took my hand and led me to the beach, as if I were her uncooperative child. She walked beside me with an air of having created me moments ago, raising me out of the sea on a clamshell. We got to the beach and stopped. I wanted to hurry into the water.

"Not yet," she replied. "Let them see you. Let them all see you…" I couldn't believe it. She was treating me the way men treated their babes, wanting the world to see the hotty who accompanied them. So this was what it's like. I hurried to the water and dove in.

The swimsuit did not go out up down my ass, but remained appropriately in place. I swam a bit then returned to my wife, who proudly held out a towel for me. She cradled me in it and pulled me close to her hips.

"What are you doing?"

"A young girl over there was watching you too closely."

"Oh really?"

"Kesar, do you have a death wish? This swimsuit is for me to enjoy and me alone."

No one felt like going to the beach that evening. Now was my chance. I wanted to test this observation and see if ladies were really checking me out in my new swimsuit. I carefully slipped them on and crept out of our rental, sprinting off to the beach as soon as I was clear. I stopped there and was just about to elegantly shake what my Mama gave me, when I heard a familiar voice calling to me from across the beach.

"Kesar! My hubby-wubby! My man! My life partner! Wait for me! Hang on! Your wife, your amour, your amore, your frau is here!"

And indeed she was. She ran up and hugged me, as overtly as possible.

"What are you doing here?" I asked.

"I told you I wouldn't leave you alone. I've now stated in several languages that you are my private property. You know how exhausting that is. You may never go to the beach without me in this swimsuit, Kesar. Got it?"

I hugged my beauty tightly to me. Just then, a group of girls walked past us, wearing bikinis similarly mini to my tighty-whities. But I only had eyes for my bride. To be clear, I didn't dare look at anyone. The tighty-whities would reveal all.

Five German Sentences

My wife, the multilingual intellectual, speaks many foreign tongues. Unfortunately most are limited to four or five sentences gleaned during her dewy youth. Italian was particularly slippery to grasp (people from our part of the world speak Slovene and, if you're our age, Serbian and Croatian, but those don't "count"). Of Italian, she began with only the ability to say the name, surname and address of a boy she'd met while at the seaside when she was still a student at a Yugoslav primary school. This Maurizio smelled of imported fabric softener (very exotic to us Yugoslav children) and wore a cashmere sweater around his neck. According to the wife, nothing "happened" between them. I guess this was due to the excessive scent of fabric softener in the trouser region.

The language that Alenka Internazionale consolidated in her youth was German. She immersed herself in the language and culture and my love sponge soaked up words with passion and admiration. She has perfected precisely five sentences, which for her is a record. However she repeats them at any and every opportunity, whether or not they are relevant, which has gotten a little old.

"Heute Abend haben Sie Gäste" is a phrase that my beauty acquired from her first German language learning cassette, German 2000s. "You have a guest tonight" is the approximate translation. She says this sentence, aloud I should specify, to anyone who asks her if she speaks German. Like the salesman at IKEA where she purchased a quilt for our bedroom.

"Do you speak German?"

"Yes. Heute Abend haben Sie Gäste," my little Heidi confirmed with a smile.

"Wunderschön," the salesman replies, before quickly turning and speeding away.

She used this same line when one of her daughters snuck into the bedroom one evening, just prior to the initiation of Happy Time. The kid had dreamed that she was in a LEGO store and didn't know what to buy. She'd woken and considered this to qualify as a nightmare. Of course, she lay down between us. That's when my beautiful wife leaned over to me and whispered in my ear, "Heute Abend haben Sie Gäste."

I never liked German.

"Willst du mit mir heiraten?" was also on her limited menu, a phrase she'd learned in her 20s when watching TV. "Will you marry me?" Unaware that this was one of her five mother sentences, the first time she said it to me, I replied "Yes." This is probably the main reason we got married.

Alenka's ex-boyfriend, who lived in Germany, is guilty of having taught the Queen of Foreign Tongues her third German sentence. The guy was always late for their dates. So Alenka asked her father to teach her the German for "You're late again!"

And so, I was served with the line "Du hast wieder verspätung!" every time I came home late from my weekly volleyball practice and wanted a slice of love cake as a reward for my athletic prowess.

German porn helped Alenka von Slowenien spice up her lexicon with two more lines. Whenever I'm waiting in front of a store and nervously checking my watch, she yells out from inside the store, "Ich komme, Schatz!" I'm coming my darling, indeed.

When I finally extract her from said store and try to get her home, she stops at the entrance to the next store, kisses me, and whispers, "Noch einmal," one more time, before disappearing within. This is roughly equivalent to Shakespeare's Henry V rallying his troops at Agincourt with "Once more unto the breach," but with a greater likelihood of purchasing frilly underwear.

To be fair, in addition to the five aforementioned phrases, there is one word that my love knows but chooses not to use. She really wants me to use it. She learned it while watching some classic Yugoslav war films in which heroic Partisans battle evil Nazis--the fondly-recalled Rambos of our youth. It comes in handy in many situations and, if used properly, it promotes love and coexistence between Man and Woman. I last used this word one morning when my hot kitten was curled up beside me in bed and gently asked me to make her breakfast.

I hugged her, stretched, nodded and said, in a cinematic, coming attractions sort of baritone: "Jawohl!"

Never Relinquish a Backpack

The security guard was relentless. I was not allowed to carry my backpack into the show, the show I'd been drooling over for more than half a year. The moment I left the hotel room, I knew I was screwed. It wasn't even my first time at a show of this scale. I've attended my fair share over the last twenty years, more than one a year. This time I wasn't going to let myself get distracted. I approached the security guard with the backpack on my back, not in my hand. Maybe he wouldn't even notice?

The wife was smarter than I. All she had with her was stuffed into her pockets...and into my backpack. The guard let her in straight away. Me, not so much.

"It's empty," I said, showering him the open main compartment which contained only a rolled-up jacket. All the cosmetics and other trifles I'd squirreled away in the smaller zip pocket.

"Not happening," he politely but firmly said, pointing to the backpack. "See if you can leave it somewhere, you can't bring it in here."

I met eyes with my bride. I shrugged. I knew I couldn't just leave the backpack somewhere. It cost a fortune since it was waterproof and so very practical. The show began in less than an hour. What to do?

I stepped out of the line and scanned the square behind the concert venue. Tens of thousands of people stood around, waiting for the show to begin. Lots of shops and bars. A huge subway station. A cinema. Even a soccer stadium.

I walked across the square to the soccer stadium and asked a security guard there.

"Hi," I chirped.

The guard smiled and nodded. "Ask if you want, but I think I know where this is going..."

"You know, I'm going to a concert over there and I have this nice backpack with me." I swung it around to my front to show him. "I'm looking for a safe or anything really where I can store it until after the show."

The guard listened politely then pointed to the shops and cafes around us. "You can try one of them. We can't help you. Maybe they can."

This rejection was anticipated. After all, this guy was a security guard at the stadium of one of the most famous soccer teams in Europe. But I didn't receive any pearls of wisdom. I made my way over to a huge store adjacent to the stadium. I didn't even ask if I could leave my backpack with them. I just saw the opening hours and realized that the store would be closed before the concert ended.

I turned to a small hotel among the shops. My heart was pounding--only 30 minutes til the start of the show. Luck hadn't been on my side. I half-ran to the entrance. I was about to swing through the door when I noticed a piece of paper on the door, as if it had been placed there expressly for me: "Only hotel guests can leave their luggage with us!" Shit.

Twenty-five minutes to go. I raced into the subway. A black van containing a police SWAT team was parked in front of the ticket booth, with five armored police standing around, sniper rifles in hand. I didn't think much of it--the concert was more important. I stepped up to one of them, then three quickly surrounded me.

"Hey guys," I said, trying to sound as with it as I could, "maybe you know if there's a locker or something around here where I could leave my backpack? I removed it from my back and they grew very still and suspicious. "I'd like to put it in a safe or something, if there's one nearby."

Their reply was brief. They don't know and can't help me. Panic sunk its claw into me. I spun around, staring wildly in all directions, searching for a beacon of hope. Anything. Whatever. I. Will. Not. Lose. This. Backpack.

I spotted a small grocery store. I sprinted in, ran up to the first clerk, the one behind the bread counter. "Sir," I exhaled breathlessly, "I have a backpack, please…"

He raised his hand. "I cannot. I know. A backpack. They recently made it a law that you can't carry a backpack or purse anywhere anymore. Sorry."

I stood helpless and hopeless in the store, imagining a hole opening up beneath my feet, to swallow me down. I was going to lose my backpack. This must not be! I need it! It's mine! I must…

I stumbled toward the exit, past the vegetable stand, past the cash registers. Then, like a bolt from the blue, my feet stopped moving. I was standing in front of an empty self-service cash register with plastic shopping bags hanging beside it. My heart thundered. It was worth a shot. At this point, I had nothing to lose. And just fifteen minutes before showtime!

I ran over to the cooler and grabbed three water bottles. I wouldn't be allowed to carry them inside. They will take them away from me. That was my plan.

I bought the waters and put them in a shopping bag. I ran out of the store and stopped at a bench a few feet from the SWAT team. I took the backpack off of my shoulders, removed my jacket from it and rolled the backpack as tightly as I could. I put it in the shopping bag. I placed my jacket on top of the rolled backpack inside the shopping bag. Then I put the three water bottles on top of the jacket which was on top of the backpack inside the shopping bag.

I walked over to the entrance. Ten minutes until showtime. I joined the line and reached the security guards.

"What's in the shopping bag?" a guard asked.

"Water and a jacket," I replied, smiling. I almost barfed, I was so nervous.

"You can't bring in the water bottles, throw them away," he ordered.

I nodded and tossed the bottles in the trash before his eyes.

He let me go in.

I then was confronted with an airport style security setup, with an x-ray portal. My wife was standing on the far side, waving to me. I smiled at her. And almost barfed again.

"Empty the bag," said guard number two. I pulled my jacket out of the shopping bag and then my rolled up backpack.

"It's empty," I said, "your colleague told me to put my backpack in the shopping bag so I could come in."

I could barely breathe. Guard Two felt the backpack and opened the outer zip pocket. He pulled out business cards and a blister pack of ibuprofen. I shrugged.

"It's okay," he finally said and let me through.

My darling and I embraced. She hadn't believed she'd ever see me again.

"You know," she hurried to explain, "I personally prevented a terrorist attack!"

"Huh?"

"I prevented a terrorist attack. There was a guy in front of you with a big bag, but the security guards overlooked him. I warned them and they escorted him out." My queen was proud. Because of her, a man with a bag was escorted out of the venue. Sweat beaded on my neck. Hm. I, too, was a man with a bag.

But my backpack was empty. And I looked friendly and unthreatening. I hoped.

We got to our seats with just a few minutes to spare. I sat down and pulled my backpack out of the shopping bag. I removed the flotsam and jetsam from my jacket pockets and put it all in the outer zip pocket of the backpack. Then my heart stopped. My fingers touched something cold, metallic. I looked around, took a deep breath, and slowly pulled my hand out of my backpack. I zipped the pocket shut, rolled the backpack up again and pushed it into the bag. The second guard had forgotten to inspect the side pocket. If they had, they would've found a big Swiss Army knife in it.

I Used To Have Things My Way

I sat in front of my house and thought. Years back, I'd sat in front of this house alone. Now the house was full. Four tadpoles and a wife. If only it were the other way around...

My thoughts drifted to those times when I enjoyed heading up a one-member household. When I was king of my own compost heap. Rooster of my chicken run. When I had things, as Sinatra liked to say, my way.

Sometimes, when I was alone, I would have only one tube of toothpaste open at a time. One that was inverted, standing on its head, with some hard and heavy object weighing it down so as to coax the last squidge of toothpaste up against the cap, thus facilitating its expulsion when I so wished. I would squeeze that motherfucker until it was thin and flat, so thin that it twisted on its own, like a torqued towel. I got every last drop out of a tube of toothpaste in those heady days past, I tell you.

But since I've joined the ranks of wedlock and created a home with four children scampering about in it, we now have four tubes of open toothpaste at a go. Two are for the little sprites. One like the tingly minty toothpaste, one does not. The one that does not usually confuses the tubes and serves herself the tingly minty one by accident. Because it has the nicer packaging. Then, upon tongue-to-paste contact, she spits it into the sink, rubs the brush all over the sink to remove the remnants, and then applies her own, which is neither tingly nor minty. The rejected tingly minty toothpaste in the sink dries on its own, as does the saliva around it. I'm always the next one to enter the bathroom. This is a trap for adults.

I blame the toothpaste company. The same company made both the tingly minty and the untingly not minty flavors. One has been used, squeezed in half, in an unsatisfying way, I might add, then someone opened a new tube of the exact same one, but which looks nicer because it has not been used and squeezed in half in an unsatisfying way. Ugh.

I used to pee standing up. More than that, I used to compete with myself to see how far from the bowl I could stand while still slam-dunking, if you know what I mean. Today, I am obliged to remain seated throughout the performance. I'm not sure how to put this in an inoffensive way, but this makes me feel like a pussy. The routine has changed, too. To pee while standing, I unzipped, whipped out Mr. Johnson and let 'er rip. Now I have to unbutton my trousers, push them along the long trail down my legs, past my knees, as if I'm going to take a dump every time. When I'm wearing tighty-whities, Mr. Johnson sticks to the twin cannonballs. I'd never noticed this before, because in my former state I used to just grab Mr. Johnson and forcibly unstick him from the twins. Now I have to shake Mr. Johnson free, like a hen laying eggs, in order to distance him from his munitions factory.

I used to have two towels hanging in the bathroom. One in front of the shower, one beside the sink. The other towels were stacked at the ready on the shelf. Today there are approximately no towels on the shelf. Girls use a different towel for every part of their bodies. I counted once. We have fourteen towel racks in the bathroom. Fourteen. And yet, there is always someone else's towel hanging over my towel.

Sometimes, when I was alone, I would watch a movie or a You-Tube video and cry along with it. Today, everyone looks at me like I'm the eighth wonder of the world if I shed a tear while watching a video of funny cats.

Recently, my beauty and I watched The Help for the tenth time. Even before the shot in which Aibileen explained about her son, tears welled up in my eyes. Because I knew what was coming. But I didn't dare to speak, lest my voice should crack and the wife should pity me. The tears would fall onto her head as she lay cuddled to my chest, as if it were raining only above her. And so, as we watched the film, they fell. I later spotted her wiping down her hair with a towel, wondering aloud if we had a leak in the roof.

I used to have one light on in the living room. Today we have many small lights. Because they are beautiful. Romantic. Also the Christmas lights, which are up for approximately half of the calendar year. We long ago ran out of sockets, so I plugged them into a surge protector that also feeds a mixing board, electric guitar and amplifier. Each night, the woman of my dreams turns on these Christmas lights and the guitar amplifier hums in approval.

I used to sleep in complete darkness. For me, it's still a luxury. Natural. The best way to sleep. But today we have two lights on in the hallway to make it easier for the wife and kids to find their way to the bathroom should they wish to do so during the night. And one light in each kid's room. But the door to our bedroom remains cracked open, so this light illuminates our room vicariously. Why? Does my beauty wish to stare lovingly at me as I sleep? Check to see if I'm still there with her? Why not reach out her lovely hand to feel that I'm still there? Go ahead, I don't mind. A little lower... a little lower...

I used to sleep alone in that big bed. Freedom. Space. Alpha male-ness. Today, I sleep with my queen. She throws her leg over mine. This means that I won't be able to sleep because I can't stop thinking about the pressure from her leg stopping my blood flow and resulting in varicose veins, and what if a clot forms there and I die in the middle of the night. Death by snuggle? Will forensics determine that my wife murdered me with love?

"Darling, you know what we were thinking," she began a few years ago, pointing to herself and the four children in the family. "You know, sweetheart, my handsome husband, we would all like a kitten, A little, small, tiny, fluffy one." She pursed her lips at me and imitated curling into a kitten-ish ball. "Soft, cute to cuddle, cuddly-wuddly..."

Four heads with big eyes nodded enthusiastically.

"...and we promise to take care of him, that he won't do his business in the house, he won't climb on curtains. And at night he'll cuddle into the bedroom and snuggle down on your chest," she continued, ever more ardently, looking deeply into my eyes, hoping for a nod of approval. I took a step back and measured them each, from head to toe. I nodded and said, in a voice that defied objection, "I do not want cats in the house. Cats are members of the natural world and so are best suited to remain in the natural world."

Having proclaimed my proclamation, I turned and walked out onto the terrace. My heart hammered. I'd dodged a bullet. Cats are dangerous. What if, in the middle of the night, a cat would snuggle onto my leg and stop the blood flow and I'd grow a clot and die? Would forensics determine that I'd been murdered by a kitten? That's not how this man plans to go out.

Miss, Can I Help You?

My beautiful bride, my treasures, orchestra of my life... No that's not quite right. I'm the orchestra, she's the conductor. I'm the one blowing and pulling and drumming and my darling guides, instructs, encourages, dissuades and waves her arms a lot. In short, one day the wife came home with a face as red as cooked lobster. In each hand she bore overstuffed grocery bags. She left said bags in front of the kitchen counter, aimed for the couch, fell there on her stomach and moaned through a face full of pillow: "Why will no man come to a woman's aid?"

I cannily retreated from her field of vision, hauled the grocery bags into the kitchen and unpacked them. I didn't yet ask her what she was referring to. I knew I didn't have to. Indeed, my supposition proved correct.

"They were standing next to me at the checkout," she said, now turning over to stare up at the ceiling, her back against the couch. "They saw I had two big, full grocery bags!" She clasped her head with her hands. "And no, no one moved, no one stirred, not a person. I had to carry them to the car. I had to do everything myself!" She rolled her eyes, turned back onto her stomach and buried her face in the pillow once more.

But that wasn't all. Now she turned back again and this time looked towards me. Instinct told me to raise my hands in defense and shout "It isn't my fault," but like a deer in headlights, I was frozen from fear.

"Tell me, Kesar," she whimpered in my direction. "What is the matter with you men?"

I masked my visage with concern. I took a deep breath, exhaled and slowly shook my head. I promised myself that I will not be drawn into this conversation, even if she threatens a sex blockade.

"If only they would have helped shift my bags from the checkout to the grocery cart," she continued, full steam ahead without requiring my presence. "Real men are an extinct species, Kesar. Gone, like the dodo bird!"

I nodded and continued to unpack the groceries. Now I felt like she'd expelled what needed expulsion. She was satisfied with her conclusion that men are dodos. And if they are extinct then their voices cannot be heard, which probably explains why she ignored my polite entreaty for two minutes of red hot lovin' that evening.

The next day, two delightful neighbors came by for coffee. The four of us sat on our terrace and chatted. The conversation slalomed from football to politics to current events, including the neighbor's recent acquisition of cauldron for preparing goulash.

"I was standing by the checkout," said the neighbor, "holding my cauldron. And in front of me stood this total babe wearing a miniskirt up to here." He indicated the lower extremities of his posterior. He continued, "She had a full grocery cart, the biggest, deepest grocery cart. And I just had a goulash cauldron in my hand."

Out of the corner of my eye, I could see my wife twitching. The neighbor continued, stepping towards the maw of the beast. "And this young woman with a cart full of groceries started to load them onto the conveyor belt and then dumped everything into these four giant bags and lifted all those bags herself and put them in her cart and slowly, slowly pushed the cart toward the exit. I felt sorry for her." He sipped his coffee.

My Amazonian warrior straightened up in her chair. I felt the warning gusts of the coming tornado.

"And why didn't you help her?" she inquired with a tone recalling surgical steel.

I stopped breathing. We actually liked these neighbors. Why did he have to tell that story? The cauldron and the goulash in it had fucked him over. He could have asked us and I'd have happily lent it to him anytime. Anything but this story...

The neighbor and his wife looked at each other and laughed.

Then he turned to my bride.

"Are you crazy?" he crazily said. "My wife was waiting for me in front of the store, in the car. If I helped her and carried those bags to her car, my wife would have killed me! How would I explain that there was a young girl in an extreme miniskirt in need of my gallantry?"

The world's best wife looked down at the ground, then at me. "Perhaps all the men there at the checkout wanted to help me," she said, recounting her own story, "but they had wives with them who would have been jealous had they done so?"

My neighbor and I nodded wildly.

"Kesar, I'm sorry," she said to me. "I'm sorry for saying that real men are extinct. I didn't even think that this could be the reason for their lack of chivalry."

Now seemed the opportune moment for me to chime in. "But honey, you're right. A real man should help you, even though he is married and his wife is in the vicinity."

Her face petrified. She leaned towards me. "You, Kesar, just stick to helping your own beautiful wife, got it!?" Otherwise you will only visit stores full of old men and grandmothers who need assistance, lest it occur to you to help some sexy young girl! Are we clear!?"

Crystal clear. Loyalty before charity.

Front Row at a Fashion Show

I woke in a good mood, full of raw manly energy. The previous night I'd played volleyball, done a few sets of pushups and situps after training, ate some walnuts, a steak and some light yogurt at home, then fallen asleep like a baby. I woke convinced that my protein-tastic dinner had caulsed my muscles to grow overnight. I checked the bathroom mirror for signs confirming this hypothesis. The scale read 88 kilograms. As I'm 191 centimeters tall, I felt young and slender. I felt strong and sexy. Ready for an event organized by my team at work - a fashion show full of cute models. I would be in the front row. The front row! I double-checked the muscles on my thighs. Ripped, dude, you're totally ripped!

I pulled my jeans (barely) over my thigh muscles. Just jeans, bare-chested, like in the ads. So I had a little hair on my back. I tried to think of a Hollywood star who also had some back hair. Aside from Planet of the Apes, I couldn't think of anyone. I would meet and watch young models. From the front row! I hadn't met many (or possibly any) models yet. Well, one. Alen Kobilica. But he is a man, so it doesn't count. I did meet some contestants of beauty pag-eants. My wife, for example, was selected as Miss Atomic Disco in the municipality of Krsko, Slovenia (at the time, Krsko, Yugoslavia) in 1986. Although there were only three girls in the competition, she did win.

I emerged from the bathroom, still clad only in my jeans, my chest bare to the elements. In one commercial, I'd seen a real man having breakfast like this while his mistress lounged on the couch, dressed only in her undies and his white collared shirt. Then man then puts his shirt on and smells her on him, as if they were making love all day...

"KESAR!"

I had dozed off in daydreams. There, before me, stood Miss Atomic Disco.

"The little one is sick, we're gonna have to get organized."

"What do you mean, sick?" I wasn't clear where she was going with this.

"What part of the word 'sick' did you not understand?"

I stood looking like a dodo.

"Can you be with her in the morning and make her lunch and then come to the event afterwards?"

What? And lose my chance of seeing first-rate models from the front row? "Honey, honey," I began, my testosterone wrestling its way out of my head, "the kid is old enough to be able to experience a modicum of independence in a time of small crisis, like this fever. What if I give her a little breathing space, so she isn't smothered with love?"

"You would leave her hungry? What if she suddenly feels worse?"

No, the wife would not be convinced. I turned to face our ten-year-old, lying on the couch and blanketed up to the neck, watching Nickelodeon. If you asked me, she looked both healthy and satisfied.

"Listen," I told her, "how would you feel if you were alone for a few hours? Captain of the apartment?"

She nodded faintly before coughing so hard that tears welled up in her eyes.

"A natural reaction," I explained to the wife, "tears of joy at the prospect."

"You would leave her like this home alone!?" my bride yelled.

Now it was my turn for tears.

"She has a phone," I said, one last charge of the light brigade. "If she's in danger, she'll call. Won't you?" I turned to her. She didn't nod. Traitor!

I surrendered to fate.

The fashion show was a success, I read in an email. A coworker sent me a photo. From the front row. Asshole. I took the phone in my shaking hands. I flipped through my contacts to Alen Kobilica. I wanted to call him and complain about the unfairness of my fate. To tell him that he's the only model I know and that, since he is a man, he doesn't count and I would very much like to know more models. With teary eyes, I pressed his name. The phone rang twice.

My wife picked up. WTF? Was she with Alen? I looked at the screen. Instead of Alen I'd called Alenka.

"Honey?"

"Yes my darling."

"How's our baby?"

"All good, honey."

"Are you calling because you miss me?"

"I miss you, honey bunny."

"I love you, too, my love."

"Was the fashion show a hit?"

"Yes, honey."

I couldn't help myself. "What were the models like?"

There was silence on the other end of the phone. I had to wriggle out of my own trap. "I mean, did they arrive in a timely fashion and behave with the professionalism one would expect from such an event?" Successful wriggling.

She breathed a sigh of relief. "Sure, everything was fine, they were great. You know…"

"What do I know, honey?"

"You know, models look like models. Beautiful, young, skinny."

Did she have to rub it in?

The Husband Returns from His Business Trip

I lay peacefully in bed. The children were asleep. The wife was not asleep. These were the optimal conditions of a night full of passion. The previous night we had failed on that front. My beloved had fallen asleep before my return from volleyball practice. I was not home therefore no sparks could fly, at least not between us. All the more reason to treat ourselves to an evening of love, kisses and mutual beneficent friction.

I rushed to the bathroom. I couldn't waste much time and risk her falling asleep. I jumped into the shower and washed all my key territories. Usually I was thorough and crevice-aware. No time for such matters now. I focused only on the points that I most wished to see visited. The shower didn't take long. I dried myself with a fresh towel, to anoint my body with the scent of fabric softener. I did not apply deodorant, so as not to obscure the fabric softener scent, a fabric softener that my goddess had hand-selected at the supermarket. Because it smelled good to her. Therefore I would smell good to her. This is Man Logic.

I stood before the mirror. Lookin' good. I grabbed my toothbrush and toothpaste. Hm. If I brush my teeth with the mentholated toothpaste, the wife might not like my kisses. She had already rejected me once due to this minty obstacle, and I'd spent the whole night online browsing toothpaste alternatives better suited to intimacy.

I returned my favorite toothpaste to the shelf and borrowed one of the kids'. No menthol. I wasn't wearing pajamas. Why should I? From the bathroom, I slipped, in my naked glory, past the children's rooms and straight into our moonlit bedchamber. I closed the door and locked it. Twice. This move would broadcast my intentions to the wife. Like a Grecian demigod, I stood before the bed, my hands on my hips, my head raised to catch the moonbeams as they filtered through the window. Let her drink in the view of her demigod of sex. That should qualify as sufficient foreplay.

"Kesar," she whispered.

I said not a word. I just nodded slightly to acknowledge her and encourage her to continue.

"What if you pretend to be my husband, that you just came back from a business trip, and you just found me in bed and wanted me?"

I smiled almost arrogantly. My girl would like to play. Yes, my love kitten. Play we shall. I stepped towards her and, in the sexiest voice I could muster (which is pretty darn sexy, I think), I said, "Hey baby, I'm home."

She stopped me with a wave of her hand.

"Not like that Kesar. Step outside, open the door and pretend you don't know I'm in bed."

"But I'm naked."

"Yes, but you're going to get dressed, because you weren't naked on your business trip."

Uh, okay. I threw on my pajamas, unlocked the bedroom door, stepped out into the hall, closed the door, reopened the door, stepped inside the bedroom, closed the door, locked it twice, walked over to the bed and said, in my sexiest voice, "Hello my queen. Your husband is home from a business trip."

My queen rolled her eyes. "But I told you that you don't know I'm in bed! You can somehow suddenly figure out that I'm lying here, that you see your big chance and you lie silently beside me. Got it? Be a little more romantic."

I sighed deeply. Geez, how much preparation is required for a minute and a half of passion? Good thing I didn't have to fill out a form and mail it in three working days in advance. I returned to the door, unlocked it, opened it...and continued the aforementioned routine, only to find myself, once again, exactly where I'd been two routines prior. I followed instructions. I slowly crept up to the bed. In the meantime, I'd undressed. I lay down in bed...

"KESAR!"

"What the hell!?" All the blood that should have been downstairs was now upstairs sloshing around my head.

"Come on, put a little more effort into this game. You just returned from a business trip, you take two steps, and you're already naked? Give some pizzazz to our relations if you want any relations with me! Get back out there, repeat the exercise. I'd like to see you slowly undress in the dark. You follow?"

I gritted my teeth. My lips dried and whitened with frustration. I'd already had enough. I would show her how things are handled! I stormed over to the closest, took my suit, tie and shirt out of it and grumped my way out of the bedroom. I closed the door and, in the hallway, began to dress as a man just returned from a business trip.

"Kamenko, what are you doing?" asked the sleepy voice of my nine-year-old daughter, who I'd obviously woken. "Why are you getting dressed? Where are you going? Why do you lock the door all the time and walk in and then walk out? Did you have a fight with Mommy? Will you move out? Can I sleep in the bedroom instead of you?"

I hugged her and calmed her down. I will not move out, my sweetie. And you will not get the bedroom. There is something in the bedroom that belongs to me, at least for tonight. I love you more than anything in the world. Now off to sleep.

I waited for her to return to her room and close the door behind her. I went back to my bedroom door, now dressed for business. I found a suitcase in storage. I found a candle and a lighter and a sexy battery-powered joy buzzer. I'll show her! I entered the bathroom and shaved, so I wouldn't chafe her cheeks mid-kiss. I looked in the mirror once more. What a good-looking motherfucker you are, Kesar. She'll be floored by my handsomeness. I blinked and set off for the bedroom. I slowly opened the door and stepped inside. I closed the door behind me and locked it twice. I set down my suitcase, stood for a moment and listened. That sound in the moonlight. I knew that sound. And that rhythm. No, no, no! Yesterday we didn't either!

I slowly grabbed the suitcase, crawled out of the bedroom and closed the door. I dropped the suitcase on the floor and took my shirt off. My nine-year-old was back in the hall.

"Kamenko, would you play with me? I can't sleep."

"What would you like to play, my angel?"

"Let's pretend you're a dad and you just got back from a business trip and you brought me a gift and it's in your suitcase." And she opens the suitcase. "There's a candle! And a lighter! And what's this? Is this a magic wand?"

Yes, my dear, it's a magic wand. It comes in handy when Dad is away on a business trip.

Sex is the Ultimate Goal, the Wife is the Only Juror

I recall our early days. The love of my life looked upon me as a demigod. Always and everywhere.

"How sexy you are when you walk. How sexy you are when you eat. How sexy you are when you laugh. How sexy you are, like a real man, not the sort with no body hair." She'd hug my face and inhale and whisper, "How sex you smell! It drives me crazy when you're unshaven. A wild man who cares for me and protects me."

I felt on top of the world.

A few years later, just before summer, she also hugged my face, sighed and whispered, "you're poking me."

I looked at her in amazement. "But unshaven is sexy, isn't it?" I'd been convinced of the eternity of her initial opinion.

"Yes it is," she replied, "until it's too much, at which point it isn't."

I was confused. "Wait a minute, my kitten. If I shave, I'm not sexy but I'm fit for kisses, probably with my eyes closed. Then I wait a few days and I'm not sexy because I'm poking you. And then, a week after shaving, I'm extra sexy because I don't poke anymore?"

"Not exactly. A week of not shaving and your beard is too long, and that's no longer sexy."

I was boxed in. I no longer was certain how I could appear sexy for my wife. I decided to test my shaving routine to determine the optimal stubble-to-smoothness ratio that would increase my sexuality-to-abstinence ratio.

Yesterday, I shaved with a razor. My dearest hugged me.

"You smell good," she told me.

"Thank you."

"You smell like shaving cream," she corrected herself.

Whatever. At least I'm not poking you.

"And you're poking me."

I gently pushed her aside. "How can I poke you if I just shaved smooth?"

"Your eyebrows are poking me."

I sighed inaudibly and found my way back to the bathroom. I have my father's eyebrows. Or rather, if I didn't machete them into submission, they would be hanging down over my eyes. Balcony eyebrows. An extendable awning to shade my eyes. My father has very young eyes because of this. Nature's sunglasses. I didn't like it, but I trimmed away. My hairdresser had once accidentally grabbed them instead of a clutch of hair from my brow and snipped them. Ever since, I've been doing it alone, and regularly. If I ignored them for a week, they would poke.

I returned from the bathroom with freshly-trimmed eyebrows. My goddess praised my marksmanship and fixed my shirt collar. She lifted it a little towards my chin and, with her fingers, pushed some of my chest hair back down under the shirt.

"What are you doing now?"

I can see your hair popping out of your shirt."

"Yeah, I know. When we met, you said it was sexy. You said that George Clooney had something similar going on."

She stroked my face and smiled.

"My naive, poor husband. It's okay. Of course it's sexy, just keep those strands hidden under your shirt so other girls don't look and drool. Otherwise I'll worry, you know?"

This explanation seemed entirely logical to me. I had noticed recently that an older woman had been looking at me a little more lingeringly than was entirely normal.

"The other option, my dear husband, is to solve this conundrum through light grooming."

"But if I trim them, they poke me and are itchy," I retorted in my manly defense.

"Of course, a woman must suffer. How do you think we feel when we groom ourselves for our man?"

I had nothing clever to say in reply. Fair enough. I returned to the bathroom and trimmed my luxuriant gray stray chest hairs. This felt somehow familiar to me, like I'd seen it all happening somewhere before. Ah yes, on Discovery Channel I'd once watched a show about farming in which the farmer used the same moves while shearing a sheep. As in the TV clip, my fluff fell in white-gray clumps to the bathroom floor. There was no going back.

Look, life is a courtroom and we must argue our case. Sex is the ultimate goal. The wife is the sole juror. I know how the world turns.

Once again with the promise of sex but without its fruition, I emerged from the bathroom, to be studied by the watchful gaze of my juror. She smiled broadly.

"How beautiful you are, how sexy," she said, practically trembling beside me, stroking my trimmed chest. "Wait a minute, I'll be right back." She jumped into the bathroom.

When she returned, she was armed. Tweezers in hand. It made my skin crawl.

"What are you doing?" I asked her. Now it was I who trembled. In fear.

"You have a renegade hair growing out of your ear."

Tears of anticipatory pain welled in my eyes.

"My love, my husband, I want you to be perfect for me," she chirped, grabbing my ear and mercilessly ripping out the renegade hair. I screamed.

"It's okay, honey. It's over. It won't hurt you anymore. You know that us girls know about pain. Just imagine waxing."

I had no retort. The only thing left was for me to hope against hope that I now really did look sexy enough for the wife.

My dearest nodded and gave me a long, passionate kiss. She grabbed me by my ears and slowly slid her fingers through my hair. Now we were getting somewhere. But her hands suddenly stopped somewhere around my hairline. She increased the pressure and pulled her forehead up, moving her lips from mine, while still grasping my head, staring at my visage as a butcher examines steers. I noticed a demonic spark in her eyes. I stopped breathing. Don't. Don't say it!

"Darling..."

I swallowed hard. Anticipatory tears of pain sprang forth around my eyes. I knew what was coming. May the heavens preserve us.

"Darling, have you ever thought about Botox?"

Men with Soft Feet

The wife and I spent the final moments of the year in bed. Dead tired, we slipped under the blanket five minutes before midnight. I pressed my cold feet against her legs to warm them.

"You have very soft and gentle feet," she whispered.

For the past few years, I've been the recipient of lovely compliments from the wife about the various qualities of my feet. Apparently, they are the most beautiful, the softest, the best-groomed. Hand to my heart, I've never been much interested in feet. But if the woman of my dreams calls mine beautiful, soft, groomed, then who am I to disagree? I can only thank my parents for beautiful, soft, groomed foot genes.

It is down to a strange coincidence on this last day of the year that I discovered the real reason why my feet are so well cared-for. Before my sexy kitten and I crawled under the blanket, just before midnight, we were in the bathroom. The wife took a hot shower. I brushed my teeth. Then we switched. I confidently stepped into the shower, but then I slipped in the tub. I barely caught myself from flying across the floor. I cursed the poor quality of the tub, as this wasn't the first time I'd slipped. I'd been thinking about replacing it for years, but I'd never actually gotten around to it. My beautiful, timid doe was frightened by my near fall and loud cursing. She leapt into the shower, approached me, hugged me tightly.

"My darling, you narrowly averted disaster," she said anxiously. "Forgive me."

I was confused. "Why are you apologizing if I slipped on this stupid tub?"

She hugged me even tighter. "You know, my love, my man, I've never dared to tell you, but every time I shower, I apply body cream. And, you know, the body cream is, well, slippery. But I do this so you will be happy with me and satisfied that my body is so soft and gentle."

A little while later, we lay in bed. "You have very soft, gentle feet," my goddess whispered, giggling mischievously. "My body cream works well, doesn't it?"

I forced a smile and nodded slightly. But I was actually thinking how lucky I was to have taken a shower all these years standing up. I'm not sure my manliness could handle a soft and gentle ass.

Raw Trout for Dinner? No, Thanks!

When I first met my love, she didn't like tomatoes. I'll admit it: this was a plus. It meant that there was never an issue when, in a restaurant, we would be served a mixed salad. The wife at the green parts, leaving me with the tasteless tomatoes and genetically modified corn. I don't recall when our "unspoken agreement" fractured. But one day, probably when I came home with a neighbor's home-grown Macedonian tomato, my bride changed her mind and heartily devoured the red fruit.

When I first met the wife, she was allergic to strawberries. This was like winning the lottery. If I could manage to hide them from my kids, I had all the strawberries to myself. I sometimes shared with our kids the wild strawberries that grow around our house in Rakitna--usually at net price plus VAT. The net belonged to me, the VAT to them. For those of you unfamiliar with European Union legislature, that meant 20% for the young'uns.

But one day, the sunshine of my galaxy learned that she was no longer allergic to strawberries. I'm not sure how she figured this out without risking allergy and unwanted lip Botox. But that's as may be: from that point forward, she's sought to make up for all the strawberries she's not eaten in her life to date.

When I first met my darling, she didn't eat fish. She didn't like the taste, they smelled funny to her, the little bones grossed her out. I offered her snails (no bones!) but she didn't want them, either. The bones, it seemed, were just an excuse. Anyway, no fish.

This was, for me, something of a handicap as I enjoy fish. So we had to steer our marriage vessel for many years with nary a juicy fish in sight. Then, one year, we celebrated New Year's Even with our friend, Robert, and his family. Robert offered to prepare sea bass in a salt crust, with mussels as the appetizer. This kind offer was doubly sticky. First, I adore fish and shellfish, but second because my beautiful wife disliked both. But who are we to say no?

So Robert prepared the meal and my dear, for whom the smell of fish is repellant and for whom bones are disgusting, consumed a kilo of sea bass and a dozen mussels, rinsing them down with a liter of wine. And to think that, when I met my queen, she didn't drink alcohol.

When I first met my Alenka, she didn't like sushi. Or steak tartare. No raw meat, no raw fish.

A few days ago, my angel and I were at a French supermarket. We required ingredients for dinner. My beauty turned to me at the entrance and said, with a pleading look, "Honey, can we have my choice of dinner tonight?" Of course, why not? Mostly because she called me "honey."

She was welcome to choose dinner, because that meant that maybe I could choose "dessert." I asked what she fancied. She shot out words that I never expected to hear, but that seemed poised like bullets to spring out of her.

"Smoked trout, my love, the way you made it for me once."

This caught me unprepared. First, she didn't eat trout. Second, I'd never prepared anything like that for her.

"Smoked trout? Are you sure?"

"My dear, I adore smoked trout, just the way you made it for me."

"But I've never made you smoked trout."

"Hello! Don't tell me your going senile already."

Okay, I thought. I tossed a half-kilo of smoked trout into our grocery cart and headed for the chicken aisle. "I'm going to get something for myself," I said. "Your man won't be full on smoked trout alone."

She looked at me strangely, but said nothing.

Evening approached and, with it, time to make dinner. I removed the smoked trout from the fridge and the chicken cutlets, which would be my side dish, placing both on the counter. My gorgeous wife, blooming with joy and love, slid behind me and hugged me from behind. It's nice to be loved. I stroked her hair. We kissed.

"We're going to eat trout!" she said, happy as a boneless clam.

"We will indeed."

"Are you going to bake it for me like last time?"

I stopped. "Bake? You don't bake smoked trout. It's already smoked. You just eat it."

"No, no, no, pumpkin," she smiled and boinked my nose. "You bake it, the way you baked it for me that time. It was so good and I told you it was the best fish I'd ever had, right behind Robert's sea bass in salt..."

"Honey," I interrupted. "Look at me."

She looked at me.

"You don't bake smoked trout."

"Why not?"

"You smoke smoked trout. Or, rather, someone else smoked it prior to our purchasing it."

"But you baked it for me last time."

"I did not. I've never baked smoked trout for you."

"Then what did you bake for me?"

I paused for a moment. I wasn't sure. Then a thought occurred to me. "I baked you wild salmon."

"Yes, that's it! Wild salmon. Isn't that the same as smoked trout?"

I leaned against the kitchen cupboard. The woman I married thinks that wild salmon and smoked trout are the same.

"No, my darling, they are not the same."

"How do you prepare smoked trout?"

"You don't prepare it, my love. It's raw fish that has been smoked. And then you just eat it."

Her face hardened. "Raw fish? I don't eat raw meat and I don't eat raw fish and you know that!"

Twilight fell over my eyes. I paid eleven euros for smoked trout. I wasn't in the mood for playing the children's "I eat it, I don't eat it" game.

"You'll try," I replied calmly.

"Not for all the tea in China, Kesar! I will not eat raw fish."

I looked her straight in the eye. Given how I felt at the time, I'd say it was visible on my visage that I was not to be fucked with. I tore a piece of smoked trout with my bare fingers and held it under her nose.

"Alenka, I've had enough of this. You will taste it. Now. For me. For us. Before I get grumpy."

She considered parrying my thrust, but reconsidered and renounced herself to fate. She nodded, opened her mouth. She tasted smoked trout. She looked me in the eye. She chewed. Her lips began to part in surprise. Her eyes misted over.

"Kesar..."

"What?"

"This is the tastiest fish I've ever eaten!"

She screamed with joy and jumped around the kitchen as if she were a balloon just punctured and zipping around the room.

For dinner, we ate toast with smoked trout and I downed two chicken cutlets. I imagine the smoked trout was good. She'd finished it before my cutlets had stopped sizzling.

We Get a Baby

As so many fairytales begin, so too does this tale. Seven years ago, give or take between a week and several months, when my goddess and I decided to be together, we also decided that the four tadpoles already in our family (two from her previous marriage, two from mine) were sufficient. We would not be having more children. The decision was rational. Mathematical. On several occasions over the years we challenged this rational decision, but each time confirmed that, given our age and lifestyle and whatnot, it was the right decision. But all the while, somewhere in the deep subconscious, this wife's emotions were giggling in secret. Mine, too, but hers more so. When given the opportunity, those emotions escaped the subconscious and scrambled towards the light.

A friend visited us yesterday. She was not alone. She came with a baby, her seven-week-old son. Some seven weeks before her visit, we got another visitor: psychosis.

"Menki, we're going to have a baby!!!"

Just to clarify, "Menki" is the nickname that was used on me when I first announced that I did not want to have a cat in the house. Since then, Menki has been weaponized: it is an integral part of negotiations, deployed when my dearest wants to arouse paternal feelings in me.

"Menki, I'd have a kitten, a little, tiny, mini, cute kitten." Or "Menki, we would all like a kitten." Or "Menki, we're having a baby!"

I stopped breathing.

"A friend is coming to visit with her baby!"

I started breathing. "When?"

"In seven weeks."

Seven weeks? This gave her just enough time to make the bed, pad the edges of the tables and smooth out the floor. "Seven weeks?

Did your friend just have sex yesterday?"

"My dear idiot, she gave birth yesterday. We'll have to wait a bit for the visit, but then…"

And so the day of the visit arrived. I took a shower that morning,a s usual. The wife stood before me, looking at me admiringly. (Well, let's say she did. Since I'm the writer here, I can invest anything, including the fact that she looked at me admiringly.)

"Are you taking a shower to smell better for the baby? Or for the mom?"

I ignored her. She didn't let this slow her down.

"Would it be wrong to ask you to distract the baby's mother with some deeper conversation so that I can play with the baby more?

I remained silent. She continued. "I'm going to move the car so it's easier for her to park."

"She's got about three meters to walk from the parking spot to our door," I replied. She's severed a manly artery.

"Yes, but the baby probably eats a lot and has the plumpest baby cheeks."

The plumpest baby cheeks? Who did she give birth to, a hamster? And what does that have to do with parking?

"Menki, would you be upset if I ignore you today?

"What do you mean?"

"I'm going to cuddle cuddle cuddle the little baby baby baby and squeeze him tight."

"But the baby won't be here in the evening. What about then?"

"We mothers are exhausted by nighttime. We need to rest."

I exhaled deeply. "You're not the mother!"

She ignored this.

I didn't bother too much with the visit myself. I moved our car a bit, to facilitate plump cheek parking. I then moved the trampoline out of the way. This was not required, but it would have been the first thing our guest saw when she parked, and the approach was more elegant without it. For lunch, I prepared three types of meat, because I didn't know exactly what this friend would like. I tidied up the kitchen, donned a nice t-shirt, threw on the gorgeous black apron I'd received for my last birthday, and put the soup on. Just before they arrived, I added butter and milk to the soup and beat with such vigor that the whisk fell apart. For the second time that year.

The visit went as expected. My beauty hovered around the baby the whole time, whispering in his ear, "Don't worry, Mommy will take care of you. And your biological mother is around here some-where, too…"

Every now and then she'd turn the baby towards me and say, "Look at Daddy. He could be your Daddy, but he's not. That's why he's still alive."

I was a cooler customer. 100% man, man. At first I blinked a little at the baby, of course a one-way glance because the kid couldn't see all the way across the living room. It probably looked like I had a strange twitch in my eye. The baby didn't know if I was blinking at him or about to have an attack. So I moved in closer and, with an overt air of disinterest, caressed those little fingers of his, soft like a boiled egg.

We ate lunch ravenously. The friend praised my meat. I puffed up like a pastry. I cleared the table, did the dishes, cleaned the kitch-en. The friend praised my diligence. The wife took the baby in her arms. The friend took the hint and stopped praising me.

That evening, my love and eye tumbled into bed. She hugged me and kissed me gently, smiling.

"Menki…"

"What is it?"

"You were a very sexy daddy today."

"You're crazy."

"No, really. I love it when you're handling a baby. I get all soft and weak at the knees."

"Cool."

"Menki? Would you like to handle me?"

I turned away from her. "Not tonight, darling. Daddy is tired. He needs to rest."

The Four Secrets to a Happy Marriage

1. We have a lot in common

The sun of my solar system and I have a lot in common. For example, we both like good coffee. At home we have this proper espresso machine, and a proper Turkish coffee pot from Sarajevo and a lot of good coffee. We treat ourselves to coffee at least three times a day.

We love nature. We love our house in Rakitna, which is beautiful and unspoiled. We love watching deer and even bears. Well, bears a little less, because my darling is afraid that the bear will eat her.

We like to sleep late. Sleep gives us strength. When we sleep, we know we'll be spending time together.

We like to go on trips. Discovering foreign lands and meeting new people fills us both with fresh energy that carries pumps through our wings as we fly through life together.

2. We have very little in common

It is true that we both like good coffee, but the firework of my nights prefers to drink it lying on the couch, while I like to sit on the terrace, coffee in hand, regardless of the weather. I don't remember the last time we actually drank a cup of good coffee together in the same part of our home.

We both love nature. My doe loves to admire it from the warmth and safety of a blanket, on the couch, flanked by pillows, with nature on the far side of the triple-glazed, locked window. I like to walk through nature and get to know her without the barrier of triple-glazing.

It is true that we both like to sleep long and late. However, my sleepy kitten prefers to retire at nine at night, whereas my bed does not call to me until midnight has past.

It is true that we both love to go on trips, but my angel is afraid of airplanes, while I enjoy flying.

3. We make compromises

We usually drink coffee together on the couch. We rarely drink it together on the terrace.

We usually admire nature together from a "safe" distance in the warm shelter of our house. Rarely are we both in its midst, rolling on the ground. Lighting a fire, cutting branches, fighting off beasts with sticks. I usually do this alone.

We usually go to sleep when the wife declares it time to do so. I'm not embarrassed to admit that I join her, because I desperately hope she'll invite me to take care of business. When that happens, as any man will understand, I fall asleep straight away afterwards. That's the only time that I really don't mind going to bed when she wants to.

We usually go on trips that are planned via circles drawn around our home on a map with a compass. The first circle is a distance of 400 kilometers, the second a distance of 800 kilometers--the maximum that we can reasonably drive in one day.

We rarely fly. She once told me that she wanted to visit New York. I nodded understandingly and promised her that we'd one day go by car. I have yet to fulfill this promise. I have not found a compass that opens to a sufficient width.

4. Sex

www.ingramcontent.com/pod-product-compliance
Lightning Source LLC
Chambersburg PA
CBHW071741150726
47998CB00005B/1754